8th Workshop on Cognitive Aspects of Computational Language Learning and Processing 2018

Held at ACL 2018

Melbourne, Australia
19 July 2018

ISBN: 978-1-5108-6715-4

ACL 2018

Cognitive Aspects of Computational Language Learning and Processing

Proceedings of the Eighth Workshop

July 19, 2018
Melbourne, Australia

Introduction

Marco Idiart[1], Alessandro Lenci[2], Thierry Poibeau[3], Aline Villavicencio[1,4]
[1] Federal University of Rio Grande do Sul (Brazil)
[2] University of Pisa (Italy)
[3] LATTICE-CNRS (France)
[4] University of Essex (UK)

The 8th Workshop on Cognitive Aspects of Computational Language Learning and Processing (CogACLL) took place on July 19, 2018 in Melbourne, Australia, in conjunction with the ACL 2018. The workshop was endorsed by ACL Special Interest Group on Natural Language Learning (SIGNLL). This is the eighth edition of related workshops first held with ACL 2007 and 2016, EACL 2009, 2012 and 2014, EMNLP 2015, and as a standalone event in 2013.

The workshop is targeted at anyone interested in the relevance of computational techniques for understanding first, second and bilingual language acquisition and change or loss in normal and pathological conditions.

The human ability to acquire and process language has long attracted interest and generated much debate due to the apparent ease with which such a complex and dynamic system is learnt and used on the face of ambiguity, noise and uncertainty. This subject raises many questions ranging from the nature vs. nurture debate of how much needs to be innate and how much needs to be learned for acquisition to be successful, to the mechanisms involved in this process (general vs specific) and their representations in the human brain. There are also developmental issues related to the different stages consistently found during acquisition (e.g. one word vs. two words) and possible organizations of this knowledge. These have been discussed in the context of first and second language acquisition and bilingualism, with cross linguistic studies shedding light on the influence of the language and the environment.

The past decades have seen a massive expansion in the application of statistical and machine learning methods to natural language processing (NLP). This work has yielded impressive results in numerous speech and language processing tasks, including e.g. speech recognition, morphological analysis, parsing, lexical acquisition, semantic interpretation, and dialogue management. The good results have generally been viewed as engineering achievements. However, researchers have also investigated the relevance of computational learning methods for research on human language acquisition and change. The use of computational modeling has been boosted by advances in machine learning techniques, and the availability of resources like corpora of child and child-directed sentences, and data from psycholinguistic tasks by normal and pathological groups. Many of the existing computational models attempt to study language tasks under cognitively plausible criteria (such as memory and processing limitations that humans face), and to explain the developmental stages observed in the acquisition and evolution of the language abilities. In doing so, computational modeling provides insight into the plausible mechanisms involved in human language processes, and inspires the development of better language models and techniques. These investigations are very important since if computational techniques can be used to improve our understanding of human language acquisition and change, these will not only benefit cognitive sciences in general but will reflect back to NLP and place us in a better position to develop useful language models.

We invited submissions on relevant topics, including:

- Computational learning theory and analysis of language learning and organization

- Computational models of first, second and bilingual language acquisition

- Computational models of language changes in clinical conditions

- Computational models and analysis of factors that influence language acquisition and use in different age groups and cultures

- Computational models of various aspects of language and their interaction effect in acquisition, processing and change

- Computational models of the evolution of language

- Data resources and tools for investigating computational models of human language processes

- Empirical and theoretical comparisons of the learning environment and its impact on language processes

- Cognitively oriented Bayesian models of language processes

- Computational methods for acquiring various linguistic information (related to e.g. speech, morphology, lexicon, syntax, semantics, and discourse) and their relevance to research on human language acquisition

- Investigations and comparisons of supervised, unsupervised and weakly-supervised methods for learning (e.g. machine learning, statistical, symbolic, biologically-inspired, active learning, various hybrid models) from a cognitive perspective.

Acknowledgements

We would like to thank the members of the Program Committee for the timely reviews and the authors for their valuable contributions. Marco Idiart is partly funded by CNPq (423843/2016-8). Alessandro Lenci by project CombiNet (PRIN 2010-11 20105B3HE8) funded by the Italian Ministry of Education, University and Research (MIUR) ans Thierry Poibeau by the ERA-NET Atlantis project.

Marco Idiart
Alessandro Lenci
Thierry Poibeau
Aline Villavicencio

Table of Contents

Workshop Program

July 19, 2018

09:00–09:10	**Welcome and Opening Session**

09:10–09:30	**Session I - Semantics**

09:10–09:30   *Predicting Brain Activation with WordNet Embeddings*
João António Rodrigues, Ruben Branco, João Silva, Chakaveh Saedi and António Branco

09:30–10:30	**Invited Talk I**

10:30–11:00	**Coffee Break**

11:00–11:50	**Session II - Production**

11:00–11:20   *Do Speakers Produce Discourse Connectives Rationally?*
Frances Yung and Vera Demberg

11:20–11:50   *Language Production Dynamics with Recurrent Neural Networks*
Jesús Calvillo and Matthew Crocker

July 19, 2018 (continued)

11:50–12:30   Poster Session

11:50–12:30   *Multi-glance Reading Model for Text Understanding*
Pengcheng Zhu, Yujiu Yang, Wenqiang Gao and Yi Liu

11:50–12:30   *Predicting Japanese Word Order in Double Object Constructions*
Masayuki Asahara, Satoshi Nambu and Shin-Ichiro Sano

11:50–12:30   *Affordances in Grounded Language Learning*
Stephen McGregor and KyungTae Lim

12:30–14:00   Lunch

14:00–15:00   Invited Talk II

15:00–15:30   Session III - Processing

15:00–15:30   *Rating Distributions and Bayesian Inference: Enhancing Cognitive Models of Spatial Language Use*
Thomas Kluth and Holger Schultheis

15:30–16:00   Coffee Break

Predicting Brain Activation with WordNet Embeddings

João António Rodrigues, Ruben Branco, João Ricardo Silva, Chakaveh Saedi, António Branco
University of Lisbon
NLX-Natural Language and Speech Group, Department of Informatics
Faculdade de Ciências
Campo Grande, 1749-016 Lisboa, Portugal
{joao.rodrigues, ruben.branco, jsilva, chakaveh.saedi, antonio.branco}@di.fc.ul.pt

Abstract

The task of taking a semantic representation of a noun and predicting the brain activity triggered by it in terms of fMRI spatial patterns was pioneered by Mitchell et al. (2008). That seminal work used word co-occurrence features to represent the meaning of the nouns. Even though the task does not impose any specific type of semantic representation, the vast majority of subsequent approaches resort to feature-based models or to semantic spaces (aka word embeddings). We address this task, with competitive results, by using instead a semantic network to encode lexical semantics, thus providing further evidence for the cognitive plausibility of this approach to model lexical meaning.

1 Introduction

Neurosemantics studies the mapping between concepts and the corresponding brain activity, bringing together neuroscientists doing brain imaging research and linguists doing research on the semantics of natural language expressions.

The task introduced by Mitchell et al. (2008) consists of taking a semantic representation of a noun and predicting the functional magnetic resonance imaging (fMRI) spatial activation patterns in the brain triggered by that noun. That is, given a meaning representation of a word, it should be the basis to predict the activation strength at each point (voxel) in the 3D volume of the brain associated to the cognitive handling of that word. This allows to make testable predictions of fMRI activity, even for nouns for which there is no fMRI data available, as long as there is some way to model and represent the semantics of a lexicon.

In lexical semantics, three broad families of approaches have emerged to model meaning, namely (i) semantic networks, (ii) feature-based models, and (iii) semantic spaces. The models of the lexicon produced under these approaches have been embedded in wider models of the whole grammar or in language technology applications and tasks, including synonym identification, analogies detection a.o., were they have been tested on behavioral data sets. The prediction of brain activation considered here is agnostic regarding the approach used to model lexical meaning, thus providing another way of assessing the cognitive plausibility of lexical semantic representations of different sorts.

While most approaches to this task have resorted to feature-based models or to semantic spaces (aka word embeddings), here *we address the task of prediciting the brain activation triggred by nouns rather by using a semantic network, thus providing further evidence for the cognitive plausibility of this approach to model lexical meaning.*

In this paper, we report on the competitive results of resolving the brain activation task by taking a mainstream lexical semantics network, WordNet (Fellbaum, 1998), and resorting to intermediate word embeddings obatined with a novel methodology (Saedi et al., 2018) for generating semantic spaces from semantic networks.

2 The brain activation prediction task

The seminal work of Mitchell et al. (2008) introduced the task consisting of predicting the fMRI activation patterns triggered by a noun-picture pair from a semantic representation of that noun. The language of the data used was English.

Each word w was represented by a set of semantic features given by the normalized co-occurrence counts of w with a set of 25 verbs. These counts were obtained from the Web 1T 5-gram data set

1

Proceedings of the Eighth Workshop on Cognitive Aspects of Computational Language Learning and Processing, pages 1–5
Melbourne, Australia, July 19, 2018. ©2018 Association for Computational Linguistics

(Brants and Franz, 2006), using the n-grams up to length 5 generated from 1 trillion tokens of text.

The 25 verbs were manually selected due to their correspondence to basic sensory and motor activities.[1] Sensory-motor features should be particularly relevant for the representation of objects and, in fact, alternative features based on a random selection of 25 frequent words performed worse.

The fMRI activation pattern at every voxel in the brain is calculated as a weighted sum of each of the 25 semantic features, where the weights are learned by regression to maximum likelihood estimates given observed fMRI data.

To produce the fMRI data, 9 participants were shown 60 different word-picture pairs,[2] the stimuli, each presented 6 times. For each participant, a representative fMRI image for each stimulus was calculated by determining the mean fMRI response from the 6 repetitions and subtracting from each the mean of all 60 stimuli.

Separate models were learned for each of the 9 participants. These models were evaluated using leave-two-out cross-validation, where in each cross-validation iteration the model was asked to predict the fMRI activation for the two held-out words. The two predictions were matched against the two observed activations for those words using cosine similarity over the 500 most stable voxels.

Randomly assigning the two predictions to the two observations would yield a 0.50 accuracy. The models in the seminal paper (Mitchell et al., 2008) achieve a mean accuracy of 0.77, with all individual accuracies significantly above chance.

These results support the plausibility of the two key assumptions underlying the task, namely that (i) brain activation patterns can be predicted from semantic representations of words; and that (ii) lexical semantics can be captured by co-occurrence statistics, the assumption underlying semantics space models of the lexicon.

3 Related work

Several authors have addressed this brain activation prediction task, keeping up with its basic assumptions and resorting to the same data sets for the sake of the comparability of the performance scores obtained.

In an initial period, different authors sought to explore the experimental space of the task by focusing on different ways to set up the features.

Devereux et al. (2010) find that choosing the set of verbs used for the semantic features under an automatic approach can lead to predictions that are equally good as when using the manually selected set of verbs. Jelodar et al. (2010) use the same set of 25 features to represent a word, but instead of basing the features on co-occurrence counts they resort to relatedness measures based on WordNet. Fernandino et al. (2015) use instead a set of features with 5 sensory-motor experience based attributes (sound, color, visual motion, shape, and manipulation). The relatedness scores between the stimulus word and the attributes are based on human ratings instead of corpus data.

Subsequently, as distributional semantics became increasingly popular, authors moved from feature-based representations of the meaning of words to experiment with different vector based representation models (aka word embeddings).

Murphy et al. (2012) compare different corpus-based models to derive word embeddings. They find the best results with dependency-based embeddings, where words inside the context window are extended with grammatical functions. Binder et al. (2016) use word representations based on 65 experiential attributes with relatedness scores crowdsourced from over 1,700 participants. Xu et al. (2016) present BrainBench, a workbench to test embedding models on both behavioral and brain imaging data sets. Anderson et al. (2017) use a linguistic model based on word2vec embeddings and a visual model built with a deep convolutional neural network on the Google Images data set.

Recently, Abnar et al. (2018) evaluated 8 different embeddings regarding their usefulness in predicting neural activation patterns: the co-occurrence embeddings of (Mitchell et al., 2008); the experiential embeddings of (Binder et al., 2016); the non-distributional feature-based embeddings of (Faruqui and Dyer, 2015); and 5 different distributional embeddings, namely word2vec (Mikolov et al., 2013), Fasttext (Bojanowski et al., 2016), dependency-based word2vec (Levy and Goldberg, 2014), GloVe (Pennington et al., 2014) and LexVec (Salle et al., 2016). These authors found that dependency-

---

[1]The verbs are: *approach, break, clean, drive, eat, enter, fear, fill, hear, lift, listen, manipulate, move, near, open, push, ride, rub, run, say, see, smell, taste, touch,* and *wear.*

[2]The 60 pairs are composed of 5 items from each of the 12 concrete semantic categories (animals, body parts, buildings, building parts, clothing, furniture, insects, kitchen items, tools, vegetables, vehicles, and other man-made items).

based word2vec achieves the best performance among the approaches resorting to word embeddings, while the seminal approach resorting to 25 features "is doing slightly better on average" with respect to all the approaches experimented with.

The rationale guiding the various works presented in this Section is that the better the performance of the system the higher is the cognitive plausibility of the lexical semantics model resorted to. It is also important to note, however, that there is not always a clearly better method since results show that different methods have different error patterns (Abnar et al., 2018).

4   WordNet embeddings

The previous Sections indicate that approaches to the brain activation task typically resort to feature-based models or to semantic spaces to represent the meaning of words.

In this paper, we address this task by using instead a semantic network as the base repository of lexical semantic knowledge, namely WordNet. We then resort to a novel methodology developed by us (Saedi et al., 2018) for generating semantic space embeddings from semantic networks, and use it to obtain WordNet embeddings. This method is based on the intuition that the larger the number of paths and the shorter the paths connecting any two nodes in a network the stronger is their semantic association.

The conversion method begins by representing the semantic graph as an adjacency matrix M, where element M_{ij} is set to 1 if there is an edge between word w_i and word w_j, and 0 otherwise. Then, this initial relatedness of immediately adjacent words is "propagated" through the matrix by iterating the following cumulative addition

$$M_G^{(n)} = I + \alpha M + \alpha^2 M^2 + \cdots + \alpha^n M^n \quad (1)$$

where I is the identity matrix, the n-th power of the transition matrix, M^n, is the matrix where each M_{ij} counts the number of paths of lenght n between nodes i and j, and α is a decay factor.

The limit of this sum is given by the following closed expression (see Newman, 2010, Eq. 7.63):

$$M_G = \sum_{e=0}^{\infty} (\alpha M)^e = (I - \alpha M)^{-1} \quad (2)$$

Matrix M_G is subsequently submitted to a Positive Point-wise Mutual Information transformation, each line is L2-normalized and, finally, Principal Component Analysis is applied, reducing

each line to the size of the desired embedding space. Row i of matrix M_G is then taken as the embedding for word w_i.

Using the methodology outlined above, embeddings with size 850 were extracted from a subset of 60k words in version 3 of English WordNet.[3] When run on the mainstream semantic similarity data set SimLex-999 (Hill et al., 2016), the resulting embeddings showed highly competitive results, outperforming word2vec by some 15% We refer to our embeddings as wnet2vec.[4]

5   Experiment

The good results obtained with wnet2vec in the semantic similarity task lead to experiment with them also in the brain activation prediction task.

5.1   System training

We resorted to the framework implementation[5] by Abnar et al. (2018). Training ran for 1,000 epochs, with a batch size of 29 and a learning rate of 0.001. The loss function is calculated by adding the Huber loss, the mean pairwise squared error and the L2-norm (on weights and bias). Like in previous works, only the 500 most stable voxels are selected. Training was done on a Tesla K40m GPU and took 54 hours (6 hours per subject).

Figure 1 shows an example for Participant 1, with the model prediction and the observed fMRI activation pattern for the word *eye*. The brain activation images were generated with Nibabel (Brett et al., 2017) and Nilearn (Abraham et al., 2014).

5.2   Evaluation and discussion

We followed the usual evaluation procedure for this framework. The cross-validated, leave-two-out mean accuracy was 0.71. The full scores, together with the scores from the original paper, are summarized in Table 1 and shown graphically in Figure 2 (0.50 corresponds to chance).[6]

This indicates that wnet2vec has a competitive performance in this task as the mean score obtained is in the range of the scores found for all ap-

---

[3]We used less than half of the ~150k words in WordNet due to computational limitations as the matrix inverse in (2) faces substantial challenges in terms of the memory footprint.

[4]Available at `https://github.com/nlx-group/WordNetEmbeddings`

[5]`https://github.com/samiraabnar/NeuroSemantics/`

[6]Materials for replication available at `https://github.com/nlx-group/BrainActivation`

3

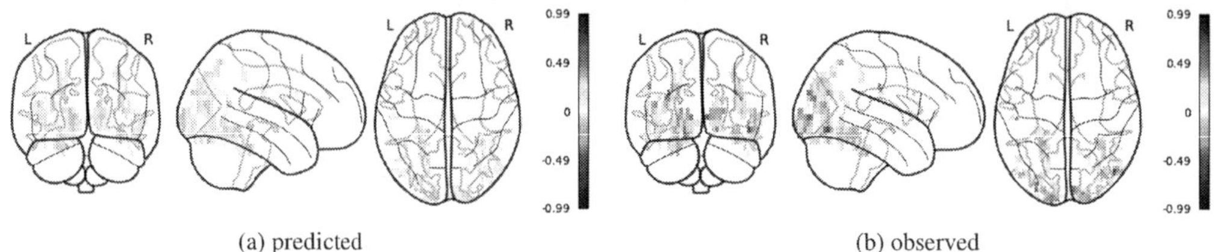

(a) predicted   (b) observed

Figure 1: fMRI activations for Participant 1, word *eye*

Embeddings	P1	P2	P3	P4	P5	P6	P7	P8	P9	mean
(Mitchell et al., 2008)	0.83	0.76	0.78	0.72	0.78	0.85	0.73	0.68	0.82	0.77
wnet2vec	0.84	0.72	0.86	0.75	0.60	0.67	0.70	0.53	0.74	0.71

Table 1: Accuracy results for the 9 subjects

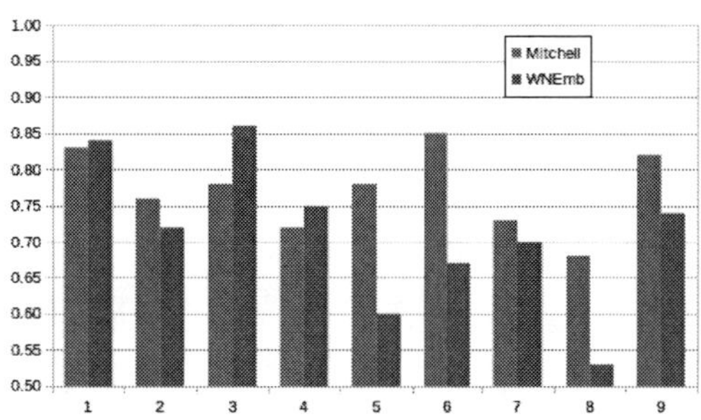

Figure 2: Accuracy results for the 9 subjects

proaches resorting to word embeddings, systematically tested by (Abnar et al., 2018).

In line with all approaches resorting to word embeddings (Abnar et al., 2018), the mean score obtained is also not outperforming the original 25 verb-based co-occurrence features model reported in the seminal paper (Mitchell et al., 2008).

When comparing the scores per participant, the bulk of the wnet2vec losses are due to P5, P6 and P8. For the other subjects, results are close or, in three cases, even better than those from the seminal paper. This highlights the point already made in (Abnar et al., 2018), that different methods have different error patterns, which suggests that an ensemble of classifiers could lead to better overall accuracy. And also, that a dataset with only 9 subjects — the dataset used in the literature on this task since (Mitchell et al., 2008) — may be hindering better empirically grounded conclusions.

Finally, it should be noted that these competitive results were obtained with wnet2vec generated on the basis of 60k words only, thus less than half of WordNet. It will be very interesting to see how the performance of this approach progresses when larger portions of WordNet are taken into account as computational limitations can be overcome.

6 Conclusions

We report on an experiment with the task of predicting the fMRI spatial activation patterns in the brain associated with a given noun.

We resorted to a semantic network of lexical knowledge, viz. WordNet, and thus to a representation of the meaning of the input nouns as elements of concept nodes in a graph of semantically related edges. We also resorted to a derived intermediate vectorial semantic representation (word embeddings) for the input nouns that was obtained by a novel methodology to convert semantic networks into semantic spaces, applied to WordNet.

The results indicate that this model has a competitive performance as its scores are within the range of the results obtained with state of the art models based on corpus-based word embeddings reported in the literature. Though for one third of the 9 subjects this model surpasses Mitchell et al. (2008), on average it did not outperform that seminal model, which used hand-selected features.

The fact that less than half of the words in WordNet were used allows a positive expectation with respect to the strength of the proposed approach, and points towards future work that will seek to use larger portions of WordNet, and further lexical semantics networks and ontologies.

References

Samira Abnar, Rasyan Ahmed, Max Mijnheer, and Willem Zuidema. 2018. Experiential, distributional and dependency-based word embeddings have complementary roles in decoding brain activity. In *Proceedings of the 8th Workshop on Cognitive Modeling and Computational Linguistics (CMCL 2018)*, pages 5766.

Alexandre Abraham, Fabian Pedregosa, Michael Eickenberg, Philippe Gervais, Andreas Mueller, Jean Kossaifi, Alexandre Gramfort, Bertrand Thirion, and GaelVaroquaux. 2014. Machine learning for neuroimaging with scikit-learn. *Frontiers in Neuroinformatics*, 8:14.

Andrew J. Anderson, Douwe Kiela, Stephen Clark, and Massimo Poesio. 2017. Visually grounded and textual semantic models differentially decode brain activity associated with concrete and abstract nouns. *Transactions of the Association of Computational Linguistics*, 5(1):17–30.

Jeffrey R. Binder, Lisa L. Conant, Colin J. Humphries, Leonardo Fernandino, Stephen B. Simons, Mario Aguilar, and Rutvik H. Desai. 2016. Toward a brain-based componential semantic representation. *Cognitive neuropsychology*, 33(3-4):130–174.

Piotr Bojanowski, Edouard Grave, Armand Joulin, and Tomas Mikolov. 2016. Enriching word vectors with subword information. *arXiv preprint arXiv:1607.04606*.

Thorsten Brants and Alex Franz. 2006. Web 1T 5-gram version 1.

Matthew Brett, Michael Hanke, et al. 2017. nipy/nibabel: 2.2.0.

Barry Devereux, Colin Kelly, and Anna Korhonen. 2010. Using fMRI activation to conceptual stimuli to evaluate methods for extracting conceptual representations from corpora. In *Proceedings of the NAACL HLT 2010 First Workshop on Computational Neurolinguistics*, pages 70–78. Association for Computational Linguistics.

Manaal Faruqui and Chris Dyer. 2015. Non-distributional word vector representations. *arXiv preprint arXiv:1506.05230*.

Christiane Fellbaum, editor. 1998. *WordNet: An Electronic Lexical Database*. MIT Press.

Leonardo Fernandino, Colin J. Humphries, Mark S. Seidenberg, William L. Gross, Lisa L. Conant, and Jeffrey R. Binder. 2015. Predicting brain activation patterns associated with individual lexical concepts based on five sensory-motor attributes. *Neuropsychologia*, 76:17–26.

Felix Hill, Roi Reichart, and Anna Korhonen. 2016. Simlex-999: Evaluating semantic models with (genuine) similarity estimation. *Computational Linguistics*, 41:665–695.

Ahmad Babaeian Jelodar, Mehrdad Alizadeh, and Shahram Khadivi. 2010. WordNet based features for predicting brain activity associated with meanings of nouns. In *Proceedings of the NAACL HLT 2010 First Workshop on Computational Neurolinguistics*, pages 18–26. Association for Computational Linguistics.

Omer Levy and Yoav Goldberg. 2014. Dependency-based word embeddings. In *Proceedings of the 52nd Annual Meeting of the Association for Computational Linguistics (ACL)*, volume 2, pages 302–308.

Tomas Mikolov, Kai Chen, Greg Corrado, and Jeffrey Dean. 2013. Efficient estimation of word representations in vector space. *arXiv preprint arXiv:1301.3781*.

Tom M. Mitchell, Svetlana V. Shinkareva, Andrew Carlson, Kai-Min Chang, Vicente L. Malave, Robert A. Mason, and Marcel Adam Just. 2008. Predicting human brain activity associated with the meanings of nouns. *Science*, 320(5880):1191–1195.

Brian Murphy, Partha Talukdar, and Tom Mitchell. 2012. Selecting corpus-semantic models for neurolinguistic decoding. In *Proceedings of the First Joint Conference on Lexical and Computational Semantics*, pages 114–123. Association for Computational Linguistics.

Mark Newman. 2010. *Networks: An Introduction*. Oxford University Press.

Jeffrey Pennington, Richard Socher, and Christopher Manning. 2014. GloVe: Global vectors for word representation. In *Proceedings of the 2014 Conference on Empirical Methods in Natural Language Processing (EMNLP)*, pages 1532–1543.

Chakaveh Saedi, Antnio Branco, Joo Antnio Rodrigues, and Joo Ricardo Silva. 2018. Wordnet embeddings. In *Proceedings of the ACL2018 3rd Workshop on Representation Learning for Natural Language Processing (RepL4NLP)*. Association for Computational Linguistics.

Alexandre Salle, Marco Idiart, and Aline Villavicencio. 2016. Matrix factorization using window sampling and negative sampling for improved word representations. *arXiv preprint arXiv:1606.00819*.

Haoyan Xu, Brian Murphy, and Alona Fyshe. 2016. BrainBench: A brain-image test suite for distributional semantic models. In *Proceedings of the 2016 Conference on Empirical Methods in Natural Language Processing (EMNLP)*, pages 2017–2021.

Do speakers produce discourse connectives rationally?

Frances Yung[1] and **Vera Demberg**[1,2]
[1]Dept. of Language Science and Technology
[2]Dept. of Mathematics and Computer Science, Saarland University
Saarland Informatic Campus, 66123 Saarbrücken, Germany
{frances,vera}@coli.uni-saarland.de

Abstract

A number of different discourse connectives can be used to mark the same discourse relation, but it is unclear what factors affect connective choice. One recent account is the Rational Speech Acts theory, which predicts that speakers try to maximize the informativeness of an utterance such that the listener can interpret the intended meaning correctly. Existing prior work uses referential language games to test the rational account of speakers' production of concrete meanings, such as identification of objects within a picture. Building on the same paradigm, we design a novel *Discourse Continuation Game* to investigate speakers' production of abstract discourse relations. Experimental results reveal that speakers significantly prefer a more informative connective, in line with predictions of the RSA model.

1 Introduction

Discourse relations connect units of texts to a coherent and meaningful structure. Discourse connectives (DC), e.g., *but* and *so*, are used to signal discourse relations. In Example (1), the connective *as* is used to mark the *causal relation* between the two clauses.

(1) That tennis player has been losing his matches, **as** we know he is still recovering from the injury.

However, discourse relations can often be expressed by more than one DC, or not be marked by an explicit connective at all (these are referred to as *implicit* relations). For example, the connectives *since* or *because* can alternatively be used in Example (1). Note however that there can be small differences in meaning between alternative connectives: *because* stresses more strongly that the *reason* is the new information in the discourse.

There is a large body of literature on the comprehension of DCs and unmarked discourse relations (see for example Sanders and Noordman (2000)), but the production of discourse relations is under-studied. Patterson and Kehler (2013) and Asr and Demberg (2015) investigate the choice of using a DC vs. omitting it, and find that explicit connectives are more often used when the discourse relation cannot be easily predicted from prior context. More recently, Yung et al. (2017, 2016) proposed a broad-coverage RSA model to account for relation signaling, and showed that the RSA-based modeling improves the prediction of whether a relation is marked explicitly or not.

Nonetheless, it is still unclear, what factors affect the speaker's choice of a specific explicit connective. Given the previous success of the RSA account in predicting connective presence in a corpus, we here set out to investigate whether the choice of DCs follows the game-theoretic Bayesian model of pragmatic reasoning (Frank and Goodman, 2012). As broad-coverage corpus analyses can be very noisy and can include a lot of confounding effects, in particular with respect to small meaning differences between connectives, which we cannot control in a corpus study, we here test for an RSA effect in a tightly controlled experimental setting.

2 Background: The rational account of linguistic variation

Natural language allows us to formulate the same message in many different ways. The rational speech act (RSA) model (Frank and Goodman, 2012; Frank et al., 2016) explains linguistic variation in terms of speakers' pragmatic reasoning

Proceedings of the Eighth Workshop on Cognitive Aspects of Computational Language Learning and Processing, pages 6–16
Melbourne, Australia, July 19, 2018. ©2018 Association for Computational Linguistics

about the listeners' interpretation in context. Using Bayesian inference, the model formalizes the *utility* of an utterance to convey the intended meaning in context c. In our case, the utterance is a DC and the meaning is a discourse relation r. *Utility* is defined in Equation 1:

$$Utility(DC; r, c) = -\log P(r|DC, c) - cost(DC) \tag{1}$$

$-\log P(r|DC, c)$ quantifies the informativeness of DC, i.e. how likely the intended meaning r can be interpreted by the listener in context c. $cost(DC)$ quantifies the production cost of the utterance. The probability that a rational speaker chooses DC is proportional to its *utility*.

$$P(DC|r, c) \propto \exp^{\alpha Utility(DC;r,c)} \tag{2}$$

According to the RSA theory, the rational utterance should provide the most unambiguous information for the listener, and, at the same time, be as brief as possible. These goals correspond to Grice's Maxims of effective communication (Grice, 1975).

The RSA model has been shown to account for speakers' choice during production for various phenomena, such as referential expressions (Degen et al., 2013; Frank et al., 2016), scalar implicatures (Goodman and Stuhlmüller, 2013), yes-no questions (Hawkins et al., 2015), shape descriptions (Hawkins et al., 2017) and uncertainty expressions (Herbstritt and Franke, 2017). In these existing works, speakers' utterances are collected by experiments in the form of referential language games. Although various types of speaker utterances have been investigated, the intended meanings to be conveyed in the experiments are commonly the identification of concrete, visible objects or attributes, such as figures, colors and quantities presented in pictures.

3 Methodology

In this work, we conduct language game experiments to test the rational account of speakers' production of discourse relations. In contrast to previous approaches that use RSA to predict the presence or absence of DCs in corpus data (Yung et al., 2016, 2017), we compare the theoretical choice of RSA with the choice of human subjects. To our knowledge, this is the first attempt to manipulate the production of abstract meanings in the language game paradigm.

According to RSA, among alternative DCs that are literally correct for a given intended discourse relation, speakers prefer the DC with larger $P(DC|r, c)$ and thus larger *utility* (Equation 2). Since DCs are generally frequent expressions consisting of no more than a few words, we assume that the production cost for all DCs is constant. Therefore, the DC that is more informative in context (larger $P(r|DC, c)$) is the one preferred by the speaker (Equation 1).

We use crowdsourcing to collect discourse processing responses from naive subjects, following previous success (Rhode et al., 2016; Scholman and Demberg, 2017). It is, nonetheless, challenging to manipulate the intended meaning in a production scenario, because discourse relation cannot be presented visually, as in other referential language games. We design a novel *Discourse Continuation Game* that induces the subjects to choose a DC, among multiple options with different levels of informativeness, to convey a particular discourse relation.

3.1 Task and stimulus design

In each *Discourse Continuation Game*, the subject is asked to choose a DC as a hint for another player, *Player 2*, who is supposed to guess how the discourse will continue[1]. There are three possible continuations and three DC options in each question. The subject (*Player 1*) is told that both players see the possible continuations but only *Player 1* knows which continuation is the target. Figure 1 shows the screen shot of one of the questions.

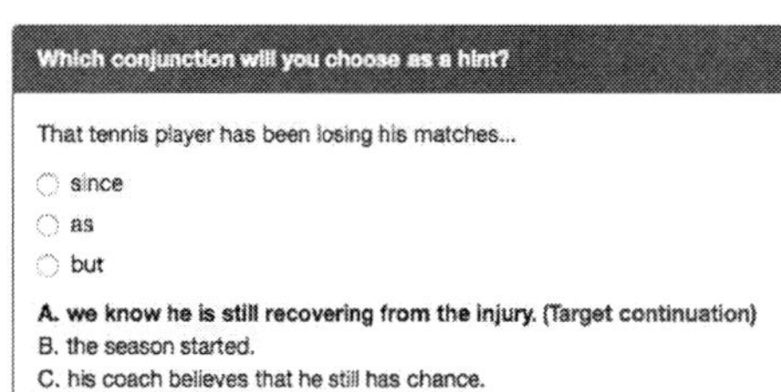

Figure 1: Sample question of the *Discourse Continuation Game*, under the *with competitor* condition. Continuation *B* is replaced by **"he was close in every match."** under the *no competitor* condition.

---

[1]We focus on speaker's production in this work, so the listener, *Player 2*, does not exist. Fake responses are generated by the system during the experiment. See Section 3.2.

Each continuation option represents a discourse relation and the target continuation is the discourse relation we want the subjects to produce. For the example in Figure 1, continuations *A*, *B* and *C* represent *causal*, *temporal* and *concession* relations respectively.

The three DC options differ in the level of informativeness in context, i.e. $P(r|DC, c)$. For the example in Figure 1, *since* is the *ambiguous DC* because it can be used to mark the target continuation *A* (causal relation), as well as continuation *B* (temporal relation). *As* is the *unambiguous* DC because, among the available continuations, it can be used to mark the target continuation only. *But* is the *unrelated* DC because it is used to mark continuation *C*, which is not the target.

When the speaker utters *since*, continuation *B* can be seen as the *competitor* of the target continuation *A*. We modify the informativeness of *since* by replacing the *competitor* continuation with another *unrelated* continuation. Under this *no competitor* condition, both *since* and *as* are *unambiguous DCs* for the target continuation *A*. The *no competitor* condition serves as the *control* condition because DC choice of a particular utterance can be subject to other factors on top of informativeness. By keeping the target identical and only manipulating the set of alternative continuations, we can control for fine nuances in connective meaning: if a connective is more suitable for marking the target continuation than another one, this will be the same for both conditions.

DC		context c	$P(r|DC, c)$
ambiguous	*since*	with comp.	lower
unambiguous	*as*	with comp.	high
unrelated	*but*	with comp.	lowest
ambiguous	*since*	no comp.	high
unambiguous	*as*	no comp.	high
unrelated	*but*	no comp.	lowest

Table 1: Level of informativeness of the DC options in the *Discourse Continuation Game* example in Figure 1.

The level of informativeness of various DC options for target continuation *A* is summarized in Table 1. When the speaker intends to convey the discourse relation represented by continuation *A*, both *since* and *as* are literally correct DCs, so both DCs are similarly likely to be selected under the *no competitor* condition. But, according to RSA theory, the unambiguous DC *as* is pragmatically preferred when there is a competitor in context. We crowdsource responses of the *Discourse Continuation Game* to evaluate this RSA prediction.

3.2 Experiment

We constructed 36 stimuli similar to the example in Figure 1, covering eight ambiguous DCs, as shown in Table 2.

ambiguous connective	unambiguous alternative	stimulus count	total
and	*also*	2	
	and then	4	
	therefore	1	
	so	3	10
while	*at the same time*	4	
	but	1	
	when	1	
	however	1	7
as	*since*	2	
	while	1	
	whilst	1	4
or	*otherwise*	3	
	alternatively	1	4
meanwhile	*however*	1	1
since	*as*	5	5
then	*after that*	1	1
when	*if*	4	4
			36

Table 2: List of DCs covered in the stimuli

Since many readings are possible if a discourse relation is unmarked, to make sure that the stimuli are valid, we conduct pretests by recruiting a separated group of participants to fill in any words that connect the first sentence with the continuation options. A stimulus is excluded or revised if, for any of the 3 continuation options, any pretest participant fills in a DC that is among the 3 DC options but is not the matching DC (or one of the matching DCs for continuation *A*). The pretest makes sure that: 1) all options are compatible with the intended literal DC; 2) the target continuation is compatible with both of the DCs that match it; and 3) continuation *B* and *C* are not compatible with the DCs which are not their literal connectives in the experiment.

The 36 stimuli (each in two conditions) were divided up into 12 separate lists, each containing 6 items. Each participant saw 3 items in each of the two conditions. An additional 6 filler items were added to each of the lists, resulting in a total of 12 different questions in a list. The order of items in a list was randomized. For each of the 12 lists, we collected 20 responses, resulting in a total of 240 native-English-speaking participants who took part in the experiment. 127 participants are females and 73 are males. Their average age is 34. 148 participants come from the United Kingdom, 34 from the United States and 18 from other countries, including Canada, Ireland etc. The participants were recruited through the *Prolific* platform. They took on average 8 minutes to complete the task, and were reimbursed for their efforts with 0.8 GBP each. The filler questions had the same form as the stimuli, except that continuations B or C were set as the target instead of the experimentally interesting continuation A. Responses from participants who chose more than 6 non-matching DCs in their list were excluded and recollected. The experimental interface was constructed using *Lingoturk* (Pusse et al., 2016).

The experimental interface was designed to resemble a communication scenario where two players interact at real time, although the responses of *"Player 2"* were actually automatically generated by the system, and were shown to the subject with a time lag of 4 seconds. *"Player 2"* was programmed to be an rational Gricean pragmatic listener, who in the unambiguous condition always chose the continuation that best fits the connective, and who supposed that the speaker would choose an unambiguous DC when there was a competitor in context. For example, if the participant chose the ambiguous *since*, *"Player 2"* would guess continuation B, assuming that the participant would have chosen the unambiguous *as if* he meant continuation A.

To motivate the participants, they were rewarded with a bonus of 0.06 GBP for each question where the *"Player 2"* successfully guessed the target continuation.

4 Results

We calculate the agreement among the participants for each stimulus by

$$\frac{Count(majority\ response)}{Count(all\ response)}$$

and average it over the items. The average agreement of the filler items is 87% while that of the stimulus items is 68% and 71% respectively for the *no-* and *with competitor* conditions. The agreement of the filler items is higher than that of the stimulus items. It is expected because only one of the three connective options literally matches

the target continuation in the filler items while two of the options are literally correct in the stimulus items. The agreement under the *no competitor* condition is slightly lower than the *with competitor* condition. This follows our prediction that, under the *no competitor* condition, participants more freely choose between the two literally correct options, because they are equally informative.

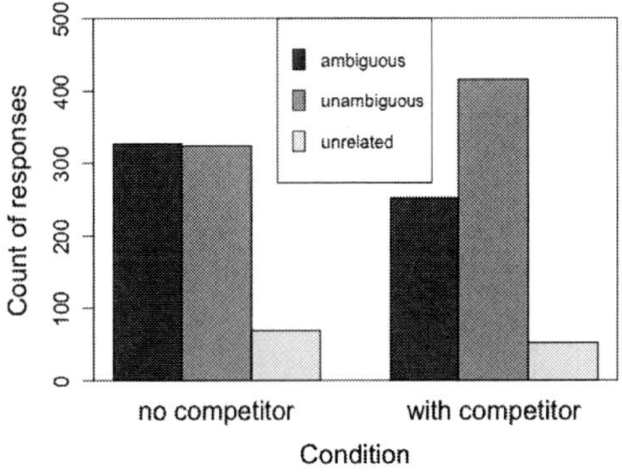

Figure 2: Distribution of participant responses.

The distribution of the participant responses is shown in Figure 2. In both conditions, most of participants choose one of the connectives that fits the target relation (i.e., the *ambiguous* or *unambiguous* DC). This shows that our stimuli are valid, because both options are literally correct for the target continuation.

Also, the results show that the distribution of connective choice differs between the two conditions: In the *no competitor* condition, where both the *ambiguous* and *unambiguous* DCs are similarly informative, speakers' choice between the two options is evenly distributed. In the condition with the competitor, the ambiguous connective is chosen significantly less often than in the no-competitor condition. This is the expected effect according to the RSA model, as the ambiguous connective is less informative in the condition with the competitor.

Moreover, we are also interested to see if there is a learning effect as the trials progress. When the subjects chose an unambiguous connective, a positive feedback was displayed to the subjects saying that *Player 2* correctly guessed the continuation. Figure 3 shows the distribution of subject responses grouped by the number of correct an-

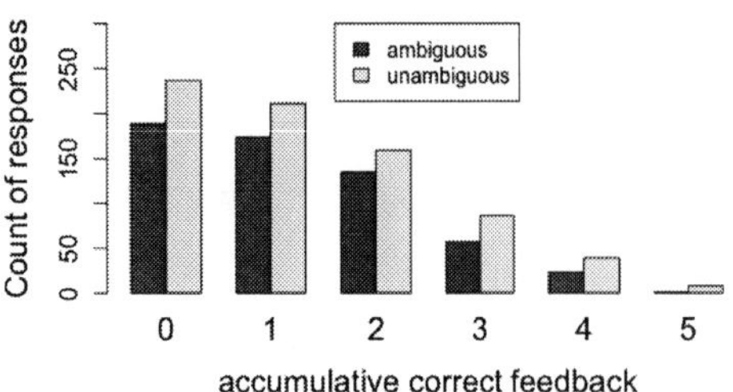

Figure 3: Distribution of participant responses by the number of previous positive feedbacks excluding the fillers

swers they previously got, excluding the fillers. Increased preference for unambiguous connectives is not observable; the subjects prefer an unambiguous connective since the first question and the tendency persists until the end of the trial.

We test for significance of the effects of the *with/no competitor* conditions as well as previous positive feedbacks on connective choice using a logistic mixed effects model. Responses choosing the *unrelated* DCs are not taken into account. We included by-subject and by-stimulus random intercepts, as well as random slopes for the effect of the condition under both subject and item. The regression values of the effects are reported in Table 3. Statistical analyses were performed using the *lme4* package (Bates et al., 2015), version 1.1-15. The *with competitor* condition was confirmed to have statistically significant positive effect on the choice of *unambiguous* DC, but no significant effect from the number of previous positive feedbacks is detected. Further investigation is necessary to evaluate the effect of pragmatic feedbacks, possibly in longer trials of experiment.

To summarize, speakers do not have a preference choosing either of the DC options that are literally appropriate for the target discourse relation when both DCs are similarly informative. However, when one of the literal DCs is ambiguous in context, the speaker chooses the unambiguous one to facilitate listener's comprehension. These results support the prediction of the RSA theory.

5   Conclusion

This work investigates the preference of speakers' production of DCs for an intended discourse rela-

Fixed effects:				
	β	SE	t	p
intercept	−.0891	.272	−.328	.743
with comp.	.649	.177	3.676	.000237***
feedback	.0679	.0634	1.072	.284
Random effects:				
Groups	Name	Variance	SD	Corr.
subject	intercept	.186	.431	
	wth comp.	.117	.342	−1.00
stimuli	intercept	2.047	1.431	
	wth comp.	.458	.677	−.65

Table 3: The regression values of the logistic mixed effect model.

tion. According to the responses of subjects participating in a specially designed *Discourse Continuation Game*, we found that speakers prefer a more informative, less ambiguous DC when it is necessary for effective communication. The results are consistent with predictions of the RSA model, showing that speakers choose their utterance by pragmatic reasoning when planning the production of abstract meanings, such as discourse relations. The results are also consistent with the earlier broad-coverage model by Yung et al. (2017), that speakers prefer to explicitly mark discourse relations when they predict that the relation is hard to interpret if it is unmarked.

The *Discourse Continuation Game* successfully extends the referential language game paradigm to test the production of abstract, non-visible meanings. A limitation of the current first study is that the alternative completions of the sentence are provided explicitly to the speaker and the comprehender, which is not the case in natural communication. Therefore, the current study only provides information on what humans *can* do, but not yet necessarily on what they usually do in natural communication. We plan to extend our work to more realistic settings in subsequent work.

Acknowledgments

This research was funded by the German Research Foundation (DFG) as part of SFB 1102 Information Density and Linguistic Encoding and the Cluster of Excellence (MMCI).

References

Fatemeh Torabi Asr and Vera Demberg. 2015. Uniform information density at the level of discourse relations: Negation markers and discourse connective omission. *Proc. of the International Conference on Computational Semantics.*

Douglas Bates, Martin Mächler, Ben Bolker, and Steve Walker. 2015. Fitting linear mixed-effects models using lme4. *Journal of Statistical Software*, 67(1):1–48.

Judith Degen, Michael Franke, and Gerhard Jager. 2013. Cost-based pragmatic inference about referential expressions. In *Proceedings of the annual meeting of the cognitive science society*, volume 35.

Michael C Frank, Andrés Gómez Emilsson, Benjamin Peloquin, Noah D Goodman, and Christopher Potts. 2016. Rational speech act models of pragmatic reasoning in reference games.

Michael C Frank and Noah D Goodman. 2012. Predicting pragmatic reasoning in language games. *Science*, 336(6084):998–998.

Noah D Goodman and Andreas Stuhlmüller. 2013. Knowledge and implicature: Modeling language understanding as social cognition. *Topics in cognitive science*, 5(1):173–184.

H Paul Grice. 1975. Logic and conversation. *Syntax and Semantics*, 3:41–58.

Robert XD Hawkins, Michael C Frank, and Noah D Goodman. 2017. Convention-formation in iterated reference games. In *Proceedings of the 39th Annual Conference of the Cognitive Science Society. Cognitive Science Society.*

Robert XD Hawkins, Andreas Stuhlmüller, Judith Degen, and Noah D Goodman. 2015. Why do you ask? good questions provoke informative answers. In *CogSci*. Citeseer.

Michele Herbstritt and Michael Franke. 2017. Modeling transfer of high-order uncertain information. *CogSci*.

Gary Patterson and Andrew Kehler. 2013. Predicting the presence of discourse connectives. *Proc. of the Conference on Empirical Methods in Natural Language Processing*, pages 914–923.

Florian Pusse, Asad Sayeed, and Vera Demberg. 2016. Lingoturk: Managing crowdsourced tasks for psycholinguistics. *Proc. of the North American Chapter of the Association for Computational Linguistics.*

H Rhode, A. Dickinson, N. Schneider, C. N. L. Clark, A. Louis, and B. Webber. 2016. Filling in the blanks in understanding discourse adverbials: Consistency, conflict, and context-dependence in a crowdsourced elicitation task. *Proc. of the Linguistic Annotation Workshop.*

Ted JM Sanders and Leo GM Noordman. 2000. The role of coherence relations and their linguistic markers in text processing. *Discourse processes*, 29(1):37–60.

Merel Cleo Johanna Scholman and Vera Demberg. 2017. Examples and specifications that prove a point: Identifying elaborative and argumentative discourse relations. *Dialogue & Discourse*, 8(2):56–83.

Frances Yung, Kevin Duh, Taku Komura, and Yuji Matsumoto. 2016. Modeling the usage of discourse connectives as rational speech acts. *Proc. of the SIGNLL Conference on Computational Natural Language Learning*, page 302.

Frances Yung, Kevin Duh, Taku Komura, and Yuji Matsumoto. 2017. A psycholinguistic model for the marking of discourse relations. *Dialogue & Discourse*, 8(1):106–131.

Continuations A, B_{wth} and C are displayed to the subjects under the *with competitor* condition, as well as in the fillers. Continuations A, B_{no} and C are displayed under the *no competitor* condition. Continuation A is set as the target in the stimulus questions, while continuations B_{wth} or C are the targets in the fillers. The connective options are in the order: ambiguous / unambiguous / unrelated.

1   Hard work is the key to success...
    [and / also / unless]
    A.   patience is important.
    B_{wth}.   honesty is the key to friendship.
    B_{no}.   you are always lucky.
    C.   you are a genius.
2   Harry was born in Scotland...
    [and / and then / but]
    A.   he lived in Glasgow for 20 years.
    B_{wth}.   his ancestors had origined from Scotland.
    B_{no}.   both his parents are not Scottish.
    C.   he would not have said so.
3   I listened to music on my mobile phone...
    [while / when / because]
    A.   I was walking back home from work.
    B_{wth}.   I knew there are more important things I should do instead.
    B_{no}.   it helped me to concentrate.
    C.   I was bored waiting for you for half an hour.
4   I will buy a bag for my son as promised...
    [or / otherwise / because]
    A.   he will be very disappointed.
    B_{wth}.   I will buy him a watch instead.
    B_{no}.   he did well in his exams.
    C.   it is his birthday tomorrow.
5   You must have been studying this afternoon...
    [since / as / but]
    A.   I did not hear music from your room.
    B_{wth}.   you came back from school.
    B_{no}.   it doesn't mean you will certainly get good marks in the exam.
    C.   John has been playing video games all the time.
6   I had been longing for a cup of coffee...
    [since / as / so]
    A.   you woke me up at five this morning.
    B_{wth}.   the teacher of the first class came in.
    B_{no}.   I rushed to the cafeteria as soon as the bell rang.
    C.   please do me a favour and buy me an espresso.
7   I will finish this homework now...
    [then / after that / although]
    A.   I will go to chill with my friends.
    B_{wth}.   I can have something to hand in tomorrow.
    B_{no}.   I don't know the answers for half of the questions.
    C.   it is not interesting at all.

8   Big cities are fun to visit ...
     [and / therefore / but]
     A.   I visit at least one of those every year.
     *B*ᵤₜₕ.   they are usually easier to access as well.
     *B*ₙₒ.   surprisingly my sister prefers small towns.
     C.   unfortunately those places are often packed with tourists.

9   Your joints will feel better...
     [when / if / but]
     A.   you do these stretches regularly.
     *B*ᵤₜₕ.   the summer comes.
     *B*ₙₒ.   still you should not start running yet.
     C.   the symptom will never go away unfortunately.

10   The older children stopped talking at once...
     [as / since / but]
     A.   they understood that it was not a joke.
     *B*ᵤₜₕ.   the train approached the station.
     *B*ₙₒ.   that lasted for a minute only.
     C.   the younger ones were still noisy.

11   Jane finished the obstacle course the fastest...
     [and / so / but]
     A.   she ended up winning the first prize overall.
     *B*ᵤₜₕ.   Mary finished it very quickly, too.
     *B*ₙₒ.   she was disqualified.
     C.   still she could not win.

12   I started to watch over my calorie intake...
     [since / as / so]
     A.   you said I ate too much.
     *B*ᵤₜₕ.   I moved back to my parents'.
     *B*ₙₒ.   I might finally be able to lose some weight.
     C.   you'd better not offer me chocolates and chips.

13   Let's just follow Peter's idea...
     [or / otherwise / because]
     A.   we will never finish the project on time.
     *B*ᵤₜₕ.   we can adopt Tom's alternative instead.
     *B*ₙₒ.   no one is suggesting anything better.
     C.   I think his idea is simple but great.

14   Maggie grabbed her coat and sweater...
     [as / while / but]
     A.   she followed the crowd into the playground.
     *B*ᵤₜₕ.   it was snowing outside.
     *B*ₙₒ.   Tom went out with short sleeves.
     C.   she did not take her hat.

15   Mark was almost an hour late to the station last evening...
     [while / but / and]
     A.   Harry was even two hours late.
     *B*ᵤₜₕ.   he was on his way to London.
     *B*ₙₒ.   he even said he was going to quit.
     C.   he was late again this morning.

16   Dave ordered a tall glass of fine scotch...
[as / since / but]
A.   we could order what ever we want.
$B_{wth.}$ the host was giving a speech.
$B_{no.}$ he could not finish half of it.
C.   Mary just ordered a soft drink.

17   Mary always wore a fancy dress to a ball...
[when / if / whereas]
A.   her boyfriend was going as well.
$B_{wth.}$ she was at her 20s.
$B_{no.}$ she did not care much about her hair.
C.   she dressed casually to work.

18   That pizzaria has always been my favourite...
[since / as / but]
A.   I like Italian food a lot.
$B_{wth.}$ I had dinner with Jill there two years ago.
$B_{no.}$ my boyfriend doesn't really like it.
C.   I think this restaurant is not bad, too.

19   My parents will visit Canada again in December...
[and / and then / although]
A.   they will visit South America in spring.
$B_{wth.}$ it will be their thrid visit in two years.
$B_{no.}$ the air tickets are expensive in that season.
C.   they hate cold weather.

20   I am sure David will burst into tears...
[when / if / but]
A.   his children come to visit one day.
$B_{wth.}$ he comes home tonight.
$B_{no.}$ Kathy probably will not react much.
C.   that will be tears of happiness.

21   Leo is taking orders from the guests...
[while / at the same time / so]
A.   George is serving the food.
$B_{wth.}$ there are too many tables for him to serve alone.
$B_{no.}$ he is not able to pick up the call right now.
C.   have patience, he will come to our table sooner or later.

22   Peter was watching the baseball match on TV this morning...
[while / at the same time / because]
A.   his wife was making breakfast for him in the kitchen.
$B_{wth.}$ he didn't understand the rules at all.
$B_{no.}$ there were not any other good shows on TV.
C.   he recently became a fan of the team that was playing.

23   Please buy some fruits for me...
[and / and then / if]
A.   come home immediately afterwards.
$B_{wth.}$ don't forget the milk.
$B_{no.}$ you still have money left.
C.   you pass by a supermarket.

24   Sam is going on a business trip to Seoul....
      [while / at the same time / and]
      A.   his children are going to a summer camp.
      B_{wth.}   he is not very optimistic about the Korean market.
      B_{no.}   he will come back with signed contracts.
      C.   later he will travel to Japan for an exhibition.
25   That task took me a lot of time...
      [and / so / but]
      A.   I expected a higher reward.
      B_{wth.}   it was so boring.
      B_{no.}   it was not the worst.
      C.   I enjoyed doing it.
26   The carnival was held on the main street for a week...
      [while / at the meantime / because]
      A.   a film festival was being held in the same period.
      B_{wth.}   it was held in the park for only one day.
      B_{no.}   the central park was not big enough.
      C.   people complained that three days were too short.
27   The cat always behaves weird at night ...
      [when / if / but]
      A.   we have a visitor at home.
      B_{wth.}   dad comes back from work early.
      B_{no.}   she was normal last night.
      C.   she will be fine the next morning.
28   The cleaning lady will come to clean our house in the morning...
      [and / also / otherwise]
      A.   she will wash the cars.
      B_{wth.}   we can just leave the dishes in the kitchen.
      B_{no.}   we will have to do it ourselves.
      C.   I think the house will just be in a mess forever.
29   The current situation is likely to change...
      [while / however / before]
      A.   our standard of living is unlikely to improve.
      B_{wth.}   the management is planning the next move.
      B_{no.}   the summer holiday starts.
      C.   you even notice it.
30   The talk will be delayed for an hour...
      [meanwhile / however / because]
      A.   the conference room is already full of people.
      B_{wth.}   people are having a coffee break.
      B_{no.}   there is a technical problem.
      C.   the speaker is coming late.
31   The teddy bear dropped from the baby's hand...
      [and / and then / as]
      A.   he cried aloud.
      B_{wth.}   he has dropped it twice in a minute.
      B_{no.}   he fell asleep.
      C.   the stroller entered the elevator.

32   That tennis player has been losing his matches...
      [since / as / but]
      A.   we know he is still recovering from the injury.
      *B*_{wth.}   the season started.
      *B*_{no.}   he was close in every match.
      C.   his coach believes that he still has chance.

33   The next concert will be held this summer here in this city...
      [and / so / but]
      A.   we are definitely going.
      *B*_{wth.}   I heard that it will be an outdoor concert.
      *B*_{no.}   unfortunately I cannot go this time.
      C.   the dates are not yet confirmed.

34   We fell asleep immediately...
      [as / whilst / but]
      A.   the moon rose higher in the sky.
      *B*_{wth.}   we had been working the whole day.
      *B*_{no.}   we woke up shortly in the middle of the night.
      C.   the kids stayed up until early in the morning..

35   We should not walk but take the bus...
      [or / alternatively / although]
      A.   we can take a taxi instead.
      *B*_{wth.}   we will not arrive on time.
      *B*_{no.}   it would have been nice to walk through the forest.
      C.   it is still not the fastest way to get there.

36   You should bring something to eat...
      [or / otherwise / although]
      A.   you will starve yourself.
      *B*_{wth.}   alternatively, you can bring some drinks.
      *B*_{no.}   it is not compulsory.
      C.   some snacks will be served there.

Language Production Dynamics with Recurrent Neural Networks

Jesús Calvillo[1,2] and **Matthew W. Crocker**[1]
Saarland University[1]
Saarbrücken, Germany
Penn State Applied Cognitive Science Lab[2]
University Park, PA USA
{jesusc,crocker}@coli.uni-saarland.de

Abstract

We present an analysis of the internal mechanism of the recurrent neural model of sentence production presented by Calvillo et al. (2016). The results show clear patterns of computation related to each layer in the network allowing to infer an algorithmic account, where the semantics activates the semantically related words, then each word generated at each time step activates syntactic and semantic constraints on possible continuations, while the recurrence preserves information through time. We propose that such insights could generalize to other models with similar architecture, including some used in computational linguistics for language modeling, machine translation and image caption generation.

1 Introduction

A Recurrent Neural Network (RNN) is an artificial neural network that contains at least one layer whose activation at a time step t serves as input to itself at a time step $t + 1$. Theoretically, RNNs have been shown to be at least as powerful as a Turing Machine (Siegelmann and Sontag, 1995; Siegelmann, 2012). Empirically, in computational linguistics they achieve remarkable results in several tasks, most notably in language modeling and machine translation (e.g. Sutskever et al., 2014; Mikolov et al., 2010). In the human language processing literature, they have been used to model language comprehension (e.g. Frank et al., 2009; Brouwer, 2014; Rabovsky et al., 2016) and production (e.g. Calvillo et al., 2016; Chang et al., 2006).

In spite of their success, RNNs are often used as a black box with little understanding of their internal dynamics, and rather evaluating them in terms of prediction accuracy. This is due to the typically high dimensionality of the internal states of the network, coupled with highly complex interactions between layers.

Here we try to open the black box presenting an analysis of the internal behavior of the sentence production model presented by Calvillo et al. (2016). This model can be seen as a semantically conditioned language model that maps a semantic representation onto a sequence of words forming a sentence, by implementing an extension of a Simple Recurrent Network (SRN, Elman, 1990). Because of its simple architecture and its relatively low dimensionality, this model can be analyzed as a whole, showing clear patterns of computation, which could give insights into the dynamics of larger language models with similar architecture.

The method that we applied is based on Layerwise Relevance Propagation (Bach et al., 2015). This algorithm starts at the output layer and moves in the graph towards the input units, tracking the amount of relevance that each unit in layer l_{i-1} has on the activation of units in layer l_i, back to the input units, which are usually human-interpretable. For a review of this and some other techniques for interpreting neural networks, see Montavon et al. (2017); for related work to this paper see Karpathy et al. (2015); Li et al. (2015); Kádár et al. (2017); Arras et al. (2016); Ding et al. (2017).

Our analysis reveals that the overall behavior of the model is approximately as follows: the input semantic representation activates the hidden units related to all the semantically relevant words, where words that are normally produced early in the sentence receive relatively more activation; after producing a word, the word produced activates syntactic and semantic constraints for the production of the next word, for example, after a deter-

17

Proceedings of the Eighth Workshop on Cognitive Aspects of Computational Language Learning and Processing, pages 17–26
Melbourne, Australia, July 19, 2018. ©2018 Association for Computational Linguistics

miner, all the nouns are activated, similarly, after a given verb, only semantically fit objects are activated; meanwhile, the recurrent units present a tendency for self-activation, suggesting a mechanism where activation is preserved over time, allowing the model to implement dynamics over multiple time steps. While some of the results presented here have been suggested previously, we present a holistic integrative view of the internal mechanics of the model, in contrast to previous analyses that focus on specific examples.

The next subsection describes the semantic representations used by the model. Section 2 describes the language production model. Section 3 presents the analysis. Discussion and Conclusion are presented in sections 4 and 5 respectively.

1.1 Semantic Representations

The semantic representations were derived from the Distributed Situation Space model (DSS, Frank et al., 2003, 2009), which defines a *microworld* in terms of a finite set of *basic events* (e.g., *play(charlie,chess)*). Basic events can be conjoined to form *complex events* (e.g., *play(charlie,chess)∧win(charlie)*). However, the microworld poses both hard and probabilistic constraints on event co-occurrence, where some complex events are very common, and some others impossible to happen.

Frank et al. (2009) defined a microworld consisting of 44 basic events centered around three people. Then they built a *situation space* by sampling 25,000 observations, where each observation is encoded by setting basic events that are the case to 1 and 0 otherwise (see Table 1). The resulting matrix encodes then all knowledge about the microworld, where each column, also called *situation vector*, represents the meaning of each basic event in terms of the observations in which the event is true. Finally, they reduced the dimensionality of the situation vectors to 150 dimensions using a competitive layer algorithm.

The language production model of Calvillo et al. (2016) uses the same microworld as Frank et al. (2009), however, the situation vectors were converted to *belief vectors*. Each dimension of the latter is equal to the conditional probability of each basic event given the original 25k-dimensional situation vector associated to each sentence[1]. The result is a 44-dimensional vec-

	play(ch,chess)	play(ch,hide&seek)	play(ch,soccer)	...	manner(win,diff)
observation$_1$	1	0	0	...	1
observation$_2$	0	1	0	...	1
...	.	.	.	...	.
observation$_{25000}$	0	1	0	...	0

Table 1: Situation Space.

tor where each dimension gives an intuition of the state-of-affairs that is being represented. For example, for the sentence "Charlie plays chess.", the dimension corresponding to the basic event *play(charlie,chess)* would have a value of 1.0, the basic event *play(charlie,bedroom)* would also have a value of 1.0 because that is the only place where chess can be played, nonetheless, the dimension of *play(heidi,chess)* would be less than 1.0 because Heidi does not always play chess whenever Charlie does.

2 Language Production Model

The model architecture can be seen in Figure 1. It consists of a 45-dimensional input layer, containing the semantic representation dss of the sentence to be produced, plus one bit indicating the model to produce an active (1) or passive (0) sentence.

At each time step t, activation of the input layer propagates to a 120-dimensional hidden recurrent (sigmoid) layer[2]. This layer also receives a copy of its own activation h_{t-1} at time-step $t-1$ (zeros at $t = 0$) through *context units*; and the identity of the word mon_{t-1} produced at time-step $t-1$ (zeros at $t = 0$) through *monitoring units*, where only the unit corresponding to the word produced at time-step $t-1$ is activated. More formally, activation of the hidden layer is given by:

$$h_t = \sigma(W_{ih}\cdot dss + W_{hh}\cdot h_{t-1} + W_{mh}\cdot mon_{t-1} + b_h) \quad (1)$$

where W_{ih} is the weight matrix connecting the input layer to the hidden layer, W_{hh} is the weight

---

[1] This vector is computed by calculating the dot product between the situation space matrix and the original $25k$-dimensional situation vector, and then normalizing each dimension of the resulting vector by the sum over the dimensions of the original $25k$-dimensional situation vector.

[2] While the model by Calvillo et al. (2016) uses an htan activation function, here we use a sigmoid activation because it simplifies the analysis, however there was no difference in performance between the two configurations.

matrix connecting the hidden layer to itself, W_{mh} is the matrix connecting the monitoring units to the hidden layer, and b_h corresponds to the bias unit of the hidden layer.

Then, the activation of the hidden layer h_t is propagated to a 43-dimensional softmax output layer, yielding a probability distribution over the vocabulary:

$$output_t = softmax(W_{ho} \cdot h_t + b_o) \qquad (2)$$

where W_{ho} is the weight matrix connecting the hidden layer to the output layer and b_o is the vector corresponding to the output bias unit.

The word produced at time-step t is defined as the one with highest probability. The model stops when a period has been produced.

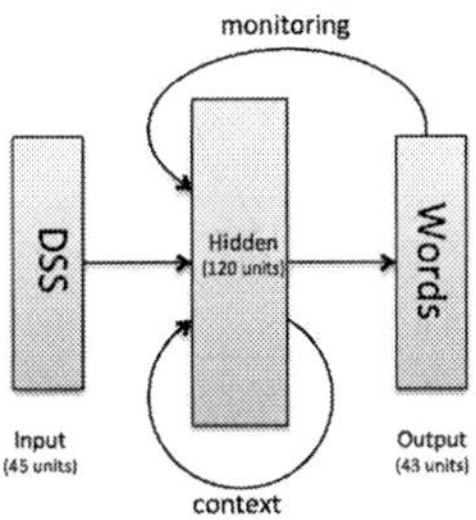

Figure 1: Model architecture.

2.1 Examples Set

The dataset that was used consists of a set of pairs $\{(dss_1, \varphi_1), \ldots, (dss_n, \varphi_n))\}$ where each dss_i corresponds to a belief vector plus one bit indicating the model to produce an active sentence (1) or a passive one (0); and $\varphi_i = \{sent_1, \ldots, sent_k\}$ where $sent_j$ is a sentence, a sequence of words $word_1, \ldots, word_n$, expressing the information contained in dss_i. Each set φ_i represents all the possible sentences that express the information contained in dss_i and in the expected voice.

The sentences are those generated by the microlanguage defined by Frank et al. (2009). This microlanguage consists of 40 words that can be combined into 13556 sentences according to its grammar. The grammar was minimally modified by introducing the determiners "a" and "the", and adding a period to the sentences, leaving a total of 43 vocabulary items.

Sentences that expressed unlawful situations according to the microworld rules, and therefore whose situation vectors were empty, were discarded; leaving a total of 8201 lawful sentences

and 782 unique DSS representations. Each dss_i is related on average to 6.91 ($\sigma = 7.13$) sentences, with a maximum of 130.

2.2 Training and Evaluation

The model was trained using cross-entropy back-propagation (Rumelhart et al., 1986) with weight updates after each word. All weights on the projections between layers were initialized with random values drawn from a normal distribution $\mathcal{N}(0, 0.1)$. The weights on the bias projections were initially set to zero.

During training, the monitoring units were set at time t to what the model was supposed to produce at time $t - 1$ (zeros for $t = 0$). During testing, the monitoring units are set to 1.0 for the word that is actually produced and 0.0 everywhere else.

The model was trained for a maximum of 200 epochs, each epoch consisting of a full presentation of the training set, which was randomized before each epoch. Each item in this set is a pair $(dss_i, sent)$, where $sent$ is a sentence related to dss_i, such that there is one training item per sentence related to each dss_i. We employed an initial learning rate of 0.124 which was halved each time there was no improvement of performance on the training set during 15 epochs. No momentum was used. Training halted if the maximum number of epochs was reached or if there was no performance improvement on the training set over 40 epochs.

The model was evaluated using a 10-fold cross-validation schema, with 5 testing conditions assessing different levels of generalization. A full report can be seen in Calvillo et al. (2016). For a given semantic representation dss_i, a Levenshtein similarity value was obtained comparing the sentence produced with the most similar sentence in φ_i. The performance was very high, obtaining an average across conditions of 97.1% in similarity scores, with 88.57% of perfect matches.

3 Production Dynamics

We based our analysis on Layer-wise Relevance Propagation (Bach et al., 2015). The algorithm consists of identifying for each unit in layer l_i, the units in the layer immediately before l_{i-1} that are most important for the activation of that unit. The process starts with the units in the output layer and moves toward and up to the input units, similar to the backpropagation algorithm.

An aspect that facilitates the analysis of this architecture is that the activation of all layers is positive, ranging from 0 to 1. Then, the difference between activation or inhibition of any unit onto another is given by the sign of the connection weight between them. Thus, units inhibiting a particular unit u_i will be those with a negative connection weight to u_i, and activating units will be those with a positive connection weight to u_i.

Having this in mind, we performed the analysis. In this architecture the output layer depends solely on the activation of the recurrent hidden layer. Thus, we will first analyze the influence of the hidden layer onto the output layer, and later we will see how monitoring, input and context units affect production via the hidden layer.

3.1 Word-Producing Hidden Units

As the first step, we would like to know which hidden units are most relevant for the production of each word. We begin by identifying the hidden layer activation patterns that co-occur with the production of each word. In order to do so, we fed the model with the training set. For each training item, the model was given as input the corresponding semantic representation, and at each time step the monitoring units were set according to the corresponding sentence of the training item. This is very similar to one epoch of training, except that no weight updates were made. During this process, for each time a word had an activation greater than 0.2, the activation of the hidden layer was saved. This value was chosen in order to record activation patterns where the target word was clearly activated. At the end, for each word o_k we obtained a set of vectors, each vector corresponding to a pattern of activation of the hidden layer that led to the activation of o_k. Then we averaged these vectors, obtaining a vector that shows which hidden units are active/inactive during the production of o_k, in general and not just for a single instance, providing us with a more general perspective of the dynamics of the model for each word.

Having these patterns, we can further infer the direction and magnitude of their effect by looking at the connection weights that connect the hidden layer to the output layer.

A hidden unit h_j having a high average activation a_j when producing a word o_k means in general that h_j is relevant for o_k. However, if the weight connecting h_j to o_k is close to 0, then the production of o_k will not be so affected by h_j. In

this case, it could be that h_j is only indirectly affecting the production of o_k by activating/inhibiting other words.

Intuitively, hidden units can lead to the production of o_k directly by activating o_k or indirectly by inhibiting other words. Similarly, they can lead to the inhibition of o_k directly by inhibiting o_k, or indirectly by activating other words that compete against o_k. Because of the large number of configurations that can possibly influence production, we will only focus on direct activation/inhibition.

For the case of activation, we obtain a score $A_{h_j o_k}$ conveying the relevance of hidden unit h_j on the activation of word o_k, equal to the average activation that o_k receives from h_j when o_k is produced, normalized by the sum of all activation that o_k receives:

$$A_{h_j o_k} = \frac{a_j^k w_{jk}^+}{\sum\limits_{j'} a_{j'}^k w_{j'k}^+} \tag{3}$$

where a_j^k is the average activation of unit h_j when the word o_k is produced, and w_{jk}^+ is the positive weight connecting h_j to o_k. This score is only defined for hidden units with a positive connection weight to o_k, which we call activating units.

Inhibiting hidden units are units with negative weights to a word o_k. For inhibition the average activation of an inhibiting hidden unit during the production of o_k is expected to be close to 0. Then, the connection weight is irrelevant, as the product would be close to 0 as well. Thus, for inhibition we do not take into account the average activation, but rather its complement. That is, for each hidden unit h_j, with average activation a_j, we obtain $1 - a_j$ and multiply it by the corresponding connection weight. The result gives us the relevance regarding inhibition of each hidden unit on a particular word:

$$I_{h_j o_k} = -\frac{(1 - a_j^k) w_{jk}^-}{\sum\limits_{j'} (1 - a_{j'}^k) w_{j'k}^-} \tag{4}$$

Based on these definitions, for each hidden unit we obtained activation/inhibition relevance scores for each word in the vocabulary. This gives us an idea of the function of each hidden unit. Examples for some hidden units are shown in Figure 2, where columns represent hidden units and rows are words in the output layer[3]. The first 5

---

[3]For better readability, all heatmaps presented here are also available at `https://plot.ly/~jesusctCogACLL`

columns show a sample of the relevance patterns in general, while the rest were chosen because they show some kind of specialization. With the exception of Figure 4, the words in these heatmaps are ordered intuitively according to syntactic and semantic similarity, having in order: determiners, nouns related to persons, nouns related to toys and games, nouns related to locations, verbs, adverbs, prepositions and the period.

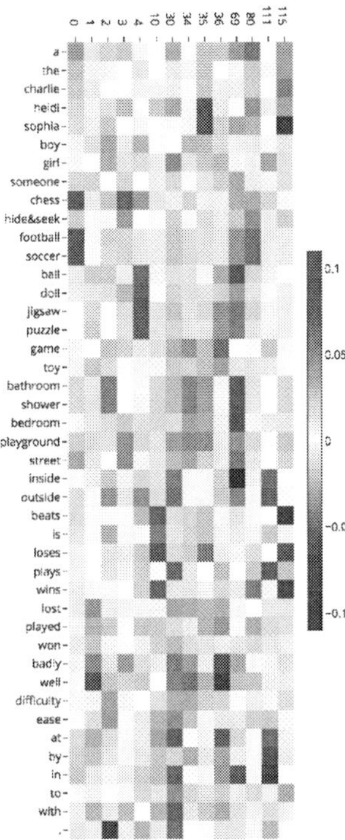

Figure 2: Relevance scores of some hidden units on output units. Red represents activation, blue inhibition.

One can see that the model takes advantage of redundancy and context sensitivity, where hidden units activate many different words depending on the context. As a result, production of a specific word depends on the combined behavior of the hidden units, where a word is produced if it receives support from several units.

Nonetheless, some units suggest a specialization (see also Karpathy et al., 2015), activating/inhibiting related words: there are units related to games (e.g., 0, 80), toys (e.g., 4, 36), places (e.g., 30, 34, 35, 69), people (e.g., 35, 115), winning/losing (e.g., 10, 115), prepositions (e.g., 30, 36, 111) and adverbs (e.g., 36).

We can also see that similar words have similar relations with the hidden neurons, suggesting syntactic/semantic categories. A clear example are synonyms, with almost identical relevance patterns, as shown by the rows corresponding to football/soccer, jigsaw/puzzle and bathroom/shower.

3.2 Monitoring Units

Having the relevance values of the hidden layer, we can infer the influence that monitoring units have on the production of each word by looking at their influence on the hidden layer.

The monitoring units feed the hidden layer with the identity of the word produced at the previous time step, where only the unit related to that word is activated (set to 1). Consequently, their effect on the hidden layer depends only on their connection weights. Then, total relevance R_{ik} of the monitoring unit i on the output unit k, is given by:

$$R_{ik} = \sum_j w_{ij} R_{jk} \tag{5}$$

where w_{ij} is the weight connecting monitoring unit i to the hidden unit j, and R_{jk} is the relevance score of hidden unit j onto output unit k, which can be activation ($A_{h_j o_k}$) or inhibition ($I_{h_j o_k}$).

Having this, we can further separate and normalize, giving activation A_{ik} and inhibition I_{ik}:

$$A_{ik} = \frac{R_{ik}^+}{\sum_k R_{ik}^+} \tag{6}$$

$$I_{ik} = -\frac{R_{ik}^-}{\sum_k R_{ik}^-} \tag{7}$$

Figure 3 presents these scores. In general, each monitoring unit promotes the activation of words that are allowed after it. Determiners activate the possible nouns that can follow them: "a" activates all toys, "game" and "girl"; and "the" activates "boy" and all locations. Nouns referring to people (e.g., "charlie") activate all present tense verbs and the adverbs "inside" and "outside". Games and toys activate "is", in order to form passive constructions. Given that locations appear always at the end of the sentence, they activate the period ".". Verbs activate words that can serve as their complements, for example "beats" activates all person-related nouns. Similarly, prepositions activate all their possible complements.

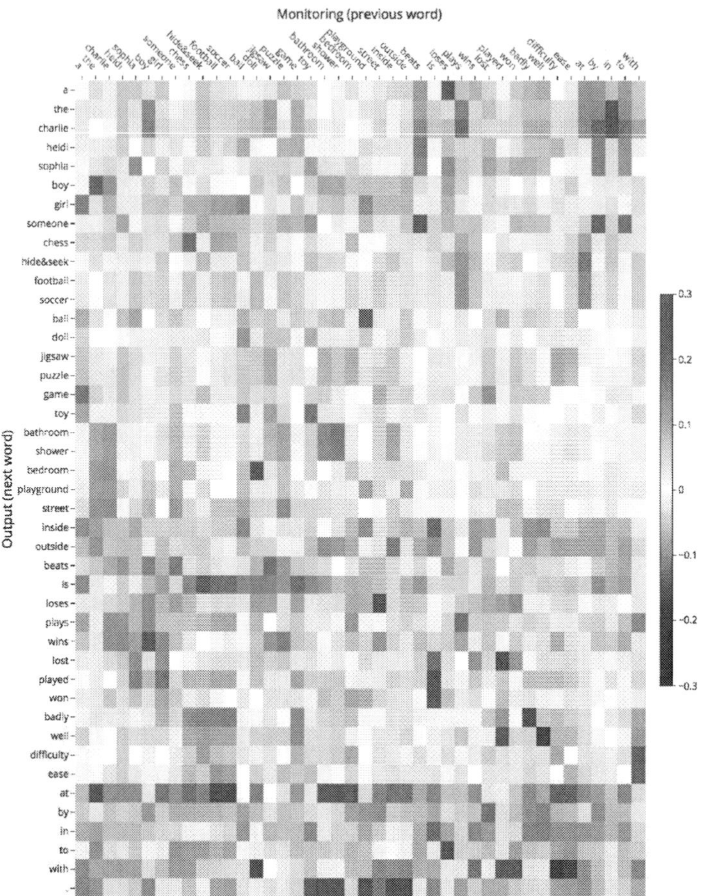

Figure 3: Relevance scores of monitoring units on output units. Red represents activation, blue inhibition.

Inhibition works very similarly, where monitoring units inhibit words that should not follow them. For example, determiners inhibit all prepositions, nouns inhibit other nouns as two nouns never occur together, prepositions inhibit also other prepositions, etc. Finally, some words inhibit themselves avoiding repetitions, for example "well" and "badly".

In general we can see that the monitoring units enforce patterns related at least to bigrams in the training set, with possibly more long distance dependencies introduced via context units.

3.3 Input Units

Using equation 5, we also computed activation and inhibition scores for the input units, where i would be in this case the index of each input unit. In contrast with monitoring units, many input units can be active simultaneously. Because of that we would like to infer not only the direction of their

effect, but also its magnitude in relation to other input units. Hence, we skipped the normalization introduced by equations 6 and 7. In this case activation and inhibition correspond respectively to positive and negative values of R_{ik} in equation 5. The resulting scores are shown in Figure 4.

In general, the input units activate words that are related to their semantics. For example, the input unit *play(sophia,soccer)* activates words related to sophia, soccer and places where soccer is played (in the street). Similarly, the input unit *manner(win,difficulty)* activates "beats", "difficulty" and "with", which are used to convey this aspect. At the same time, each input unit inhibits words that are in conflict with its semantics. For example, the unit *play(charlie,hide&seek)* inhibits words concerning other games and the place where that game is not allowed (in the street). This behavior of activation and inhibition can be seen to

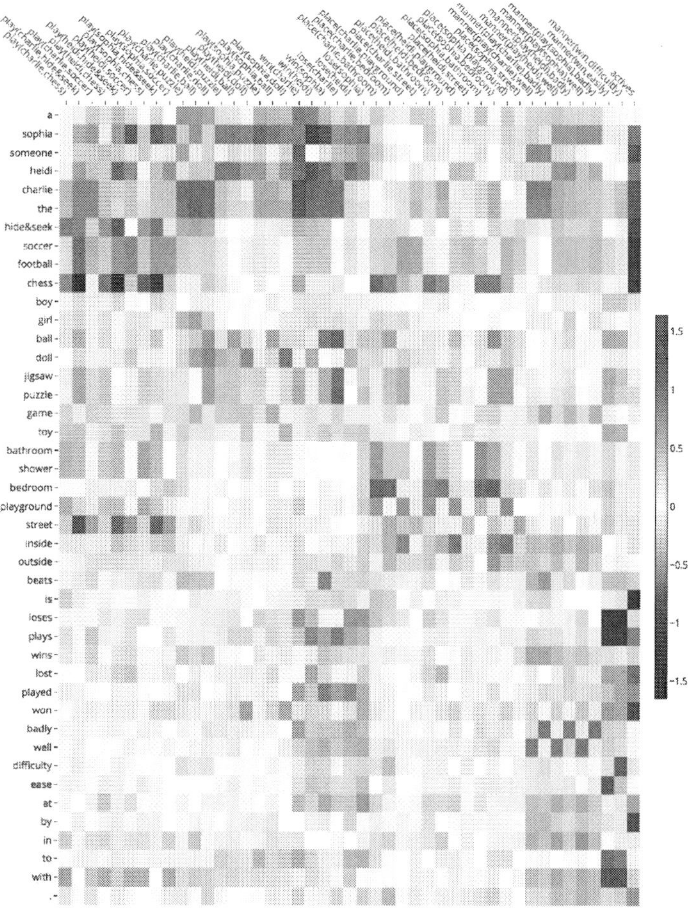

Figure 4: Relevance scores of input units on output units. Red represents activation, blue inhibition.

some degree in all input units.

Of special interest is the last input unit (*actives* in Figure 4), which marks whether the model should produce an active or a passive sentence. When this unit is active, words concerning people are activated (e.g., "charlie", "someone", "heidi"); at the same time, this unit inhibits words concerning games and passive constructions (e.g., "chess", "hide&seek", "is", "by"). Thus, production of active or passive constructions seems to be determined by giving relatively more activation to words related to people for actives, or games for passives. This seems to reflect experimental evidence that shows that more conceptually available elements are placed in more prominent grammatical roles (Bock and Warren, 1985; Ferreira, 1994). In this case, the *actives* unit learns to promote the activation of hidden units related to specific concepts depending on the voice of the sentence to be produced.

At time step 0, the activation of monitoring and context units is equal to 0. Consequently, the activation of the hidden layer at this point only depends on the input semantic representation. Then, we would expect that the input units should activate more the words that can appear at the beginning of a sentence, relative to other words. This would ensure that the words starting a sentence are correct, afterwards, monitoring and context units would be able to enforce syntactic and semantic sequential constraints, such that the resulting sentence is coherent. The words shown in Figure 4 are ordered similarly to the other figures, except that the first 10 words are those that can appear at the beginning of a sentence. As one can see, those words receive relatively more activation/inhibition than the rest. Furthermore, the *actives* unit has a very strong relevance, such that when an active sentence is queried, the words that can start an active sentence are more activated.

In sum, the input units influence production by activating hidden units that are related to the semantics that is to be encoded, while additionally giving an idea of the word order that they should follow, specially at time step 0.

3.4 Context Units

At each time step, context units feed the hidden layer with its own activation at the previous time step, providing the model with some kind of memory over possibly unlimited time steps.

We will use the notation h_i to refer to a hidden unit i in the hidden layer, and c_i to refer to the corresponding context unit which contains the activation of h_i at the previous time step.

A way to preserve information over time is by reverberating activation over different time steps. For example, if the hidden unit h_a gets active, then the corresponding context unit c_a will be active at the next time step; if the weight connecting c_a to h_a is such that the activation of c_a causes the activation of h_a, then this would form a cycle in which h_a will be active indefinitely or until other units introduce inhibition, breaking the cycle.

We analyzed the connection weights between the context and hidden layers in order to see if these cycles were present. In such cases, the effect of h_a in the current time step would be similar to the effect of c_a in the next time step. Thus, for each pair (h_i, c_i), if the effect of c_i is similar to the one of h_i, it would mean that c_i is mainly activating h_i or units similar to h_i, forming a cycle. Note that if c_i does not activate h_i directly but other units similar to h_i, it would mean that while the activation of the specific unit might not be preserved, the model would still remain in the same area within the hidden space.

As example, for the first 15 hidden units Figure 5 presents these values. For each pair of columns, the first column represents the direct effect of each hidden unit on the output, identical to the values in Figure 2, but normalized for each hidden unit; the second column represents the effect of the corresponding context unit at the next time step, calculated using the equations 5-7, where in this case i is the index of each context unit.

The column of the right side (DimCorr) presents for all hidden units, the correlations between the relevance values of the hidden units and the rel-

Figure 5: Relevance scores of hidden and context units. Right: correlations for each word between the relevance values of the hidden units and the context units. Bottom: correlations between all relevance values of each hidden unit and the corresponding context unit.

evance values of the context units, related only to each specific word; intuitively showing the degree to which activation related to each word is preserved by all hidden units. The results suggest that the context units tend to preserve activation related to most words, but to different degrees, where activation of words related to toys, locations and adverbs is preserved more than activation of words related to people. Out of the 43 words, 11 presented moderate correlation ($0.4 \leq r < 0.6, n = 120, p < 0.00001$), and 15 weak correlation ($0.2 \leq r < 0.4, n = 120, p < 0.11$).

The row at the bottom (UnitCorr) presents correlations between all the relevance values of each hidden unit and the corresponding context unit, that is, between the values of the two columns above. As we can see, some units seem to behave like memory, while others seem to erase their content. For example, units 2, 3, 4, 5, 8, 10 and 14 have a high correlation between the hidden and context relevances, implying a cycle as described above, while units 9 and 11 present an anticorrelation, which means that the context unit is actually inhibiting its corresponding hidden unit. Out of the 120 context units, 14 presented strong correlation ($r \geq 0.6, n = 43, p < 0.00001$), 26 moderate correlation ($0.4 \leq r < 0.6, n = 43, p < 0.006$) and 20 weak correlation ($0.2 \leq r < 0.4, n = 43, p < 0.2$). Regarding anticorrelation, there were 3 units with moderate anticorrelation ($-0.6 \leq r < -0.4, n = 43, p < 0.0036$) and 6 with weak anticorrelation ($-0.4 \leq r < -0.2, n = 43, p < 0.2$).

As we can see, about half of the context units have a tendency to preserve their activation, which varies according to each unit, and to the kind of information. This suggests a tangible mechanism that preserves information over time, which in the case of language is necessary in order to enforce long distance dependencies.

4 Discussion

In the above sections we separated the language production model into its different modules in order to see their function. Trying to integrate these parts into a global explanation of the internal mechanics of the model, we arrive to the following: production starts when the model is fed a semantic representation at time step 0. At this point, the semantic representation is the only source of information. Based on it, the model must produce a word that is in accordance to the semantics and that is syntactically plausible for the beginning of the sentence. As we saw, the input units seem to select the words necessary for production, and depending on the voice expected (active or passive) more activation is given to the words that can fulfill the first position. After the initial word has been produced, monitoring and context units gain influence. Monitoring units promote the production of words that can follow the previous word, and inhibit words that should not follow. At the same time, context units keep information regarding previous and current activation, suggesting a sort of memory, where information remains latent until the right time to be produced. This happens until a period is produced, which halts production.

Considering the high architectural similarity of the model of Calvillo et al. (2016) with other models of human language production (e.g., Dell et al., 1993; Chang et al., 1997), we expect that these results would also reflect their internal mechanics. Furthermore, some models used in com-putational linguistics also present an architecture where the main paths of computation are largely similar to the ones presented here: in language models, at each time step the word previously produced is fed to a recurrence that in turn feeds another layer yielding a probability distribution over the vocabulary (e.g., Mikolov et al., 2010); additionally, a semantics is fed into the recurrence in semantically conditioned models, such as some used in machine translation (e.g., Sutskever et al., 2014) or image caption generation (e.g., Chen and Lawrence Zitnick, 2015). One could argue that larger language models implement more complex interactions because of their higher dimensionality or the use of more complex hidden units such as LSTM (Hochreiter and Schmidhuber, 1997) or GRU (Cho et al., 2014). Nonetheless, the individual results presented here are coherent with previous findings on larger architectures (for example, similar words are known to have similar word embeddings), suggesting that these results can be generalized to such models.

While some adaptation might be needed for larger models, the algorithm described above might serve as intuition of how those models work, and the methodology outlined here could serve to test such a hypothesis in future work.

5 Conclusion

We presented an analysis of the internal mechanism of a model of language production that uses a recurrent neural network at its core. The results show clear patterns of computation that permit to infer its internal mechanism. Because of architectural similarity, we expect that this mechanism could be generalized to other models of human language production (e.g., Dell et al., 1993; Chang et al., 1997), as well as models in computational linguistics, such as those used in language modeling (e.g., Mikolov et al., 2010) or machine translation (e.g., Sutskever et al., 2014). In future work, the methodology outlined here could also serve to test such a hypothesis.

Acknowledgments

This work was supported by DFG collaborative research center SFB 1102 'Information Density and Linguistic Encoding'. The first author was additionally supported by National Science Foundation grant BCS-1734304.

References

Leila Arras, Franziska Horn, Grégoire Montavon, Klaus-Robert Müller, and Wojciech Samek. 2016. Explaining predictions of non-linear classifiers in nlp. *arXiv preprint arXiv:1606.07298*.

Sebastian Bach, Alexander Binder, Grégoire Montavon, Frederick Klauschen, Klaus-Robert Müller, and Wojciech Samek. 2015. On pixel-wise explanations for non-linear classifier decisions by layer-wise relevance propagation. *PloS one*, 10(7):e0130140.

J Kathryn Bock and Richard K Warren. 1985. Conceptual accessibility and syntactic structure in sentence formulation. *Cognition*, 21(1):47–67.

Harm Brouwer. 2014. *The Electrophysiology of Language Comprehension: A Neurocomputational Model*. Ph.D. thesis, University of Groningen.

Jesús Calvillo, Harm Brouwer, and Matthew W Crocker. 2016. Connectionist semantic systematicity in language production. In *Proceedings of the 38th Annual Conference of the Cognitive Science Society*. Austin, TX: Cognitive Science Society.

Franklin Chang, Gary S Dell, and Kathryn Bock. 2006. Becoming syntactic. *Psychological review*, 113(2):234.

Franklin Chang, Zenzi M Griffin, Gary S Dell, and Kathryn Bock. 1997. Modeling structural priming as implicit learning. *Computational Psycholinguistics, Berkeley, CA*, 29:392–417.

Xinlei Chen and C Lawrence Zitnick. 2015. Mind's eye: A recurrent visual representation for image caption generation. In *Proceedings of the IEEE conference on computer vision and pattern recognition*, pages 2422–2431.

Kyunghyun Cho, Bart van Merrienboer, Çaglar Gülçehre, Fethi Bougares, Holger Schwenk, and Yoshua Bengio. 2014. Learning phrase representations using RNN encoder-decoder for statistical machine translation. *CoRR*, abs/1406.1078.

Gary S Dell, Cornell Juliano, and Anita Govindjee. 1993. Structure and content in language production: A theory of frame constraints in phonological speech errors. *Cognitive Science*, 17(2):149–195.

Yanzhuo Ding, Yang Liu, Huanbo Luan, and Maosong Sun. 2017. Visualizing and understanding neural machine translation. In *Proceedings of the 55th Annual Meeting of the Association for Computational Linguistics (Volume 1: Long Papers)*, volume 1, pages 1150–1159.

Jeffrey L Elman. 1990. Finding structure in time. *Cognitive Science*, 14(2):179–211.

Fernanda Ferreira. 1994. Choice of passive voice is affected by verb type and animacy. *Journal of Memory and Language*, 33(6):715–736.

Stefan L Frank, Willem FG Haselager, and Iris van Rooij. 2009. Connectionist semantic systematicity. *Cognition*, 110(3):358–379.

Stefan L Frank, Mathieu Koppen, Leo GM Noordman, and Wietske Vonk. 2003. Modeling knowledge-based inferences in story comprehension. *Cognitive Science*, 27(6):875–910.

Sepp Hochreiter and Jürgen Schmidhuber. 1997. Long short-term memory. *Neural computation*, 9(8):1735–1780.

Akos Kádár, Grzegorz Chrupała, and Afra Alishahi. 2017. Representation of linguistic form and function in recurrent neural networks. *Computational Linguistics*, 43(4):761–780.

Andrej Karpathy, Justin Johnson, and Fei-Fei Li. 2015. Visualizing and understanding recurrent networks. *CoRR*, abs/1506.02078.

Jiwei Li, Xinlei Chen, Eduard Hovy, and Dan Jurafsky. 2015. Visualizing and understanding neural models in nlp. *arXiv preprint arXiv:1506.01066*.

Tomas Mikolov, Martin Karafit, Lukas Burget, Jan Cernock, and Sanjeev Khudanpur. 2010. Recurrent neural network based language model. In *Interspeech*, volume 2, page 3.

Grégoire Montavon, Wojciech Samek, and Klaus-Robert Müller. 2017. Methods for interpreting and understanding deep neural networks. *arXiv preprint arXiv:1706.07979*.

Milena Rabovsky, Steven S Hansen, and James L Mc-Clelland. 2016. N400 amplitudes reflect change in a probabilistic representation of meaning: Evidence from a connectionist model. In *Proceedings of the 38th Annual Conference of the Cognitive Science Society. Austin, TX: Cognitive Science Society*.

David E Rumelhart, Geoffrey E Hinton, and Ronald J Williams. 1986. Learning representations by back-propagating errors. *nature*, 323(6088):533.

Hava T Siegelmann. 2012. *Neural networks and analog computation: beyond the Turing limit*. Springer Science & Business Media.

Hava T Siegelmann and Eduardo D Sontag. 1995. On the computational power of neural nets. *Journal of computer and system sciences*, 50(1):132–150.

Ilya Sutskever, Oriol Vinyals, and Quoc V Le. 2014. Sequence to sequence learning with neural networks. In *Advances in neural information processing systems*, pages 3104–3112.

Multi-glance Reading Model for Text Understanding

Pengcheng Zhu[1,2], Yujiu Yang[1], Wenqiang Gao[1], and Yi Liu[2]
Graduate School at Shenzhen, Tsinghua University[1]
Peking University Shenzhen Institute[2]
zhupc15@mails.tsinghua.edu.cn, yang.yujiu@sz.tsinghua.edu.cn,
gwq16@mails.tsinghua.edu.cn, eeyliu@gmail.com

Abstract

In recent years, a variety of recurrent neural networks have been proposed, e.g LST-M, however, existing models only read the text once, it cannot describe the situation of repeated reading in reading comprehension. In fact, when reading or analyzing a text, we may read the text several times rather than once if we couldn't well understand it. So, how to model this kind of the reading behavior? To address the issue, we propose a multi-glance mechanism (MG-M) for modeling the habit of reading behavior. In the proposed framework, the actual reading process can be fully simulated, and then the obtained information can be consistent with the task. Based on the multi-glance mechanism, we design two types of recurrent neural network models for repeated reading: Glance Cell Model (GCM) and Glance Gate Model (GGM). Visualization analysis of the GCM and the GGM demonstrates the effectiveness of multi-glance mechanisms. Experiments results on the large-scale datasets show that the proposed methods can achieve better performance.

1 Introduction

Text understanding is one of the fundamental tasks in Natural Language Processing areas. These years we have seen significant progress in applying neural networks to text analysis applications. Recurrent neural network is widely used because of its effective capability of capturing the sequential information. Long short-term memory (LST-M) (Hochreiter and Schmidhuber, 1997) and gated recurrent neural network (Chung et al., 2014) have achieved state-of-the-art performance in many ar-

eas, such as sentiment analysis (Tang et al., 2014; Chen et al., 2016), document classification (Yang et al., 2016) and neural machine translation (Bahdanau et al., 2014). Besides the success achieved by these basic recurrent neural models, there are also a lot of interesting research works conducted in text analysis (Kim, 2014; Zhang et al., 2015). Depending on the parsing tree structures, tree-LSTM (Tai et al., 2015) and recursive neural network(Socher et al., 2013) are proposed. Bidirectional recurrent neural networks (Schuster and Paliwal, 1997) can get the backward features. In order to align the hidden states, attention mechanism is widely used in language processing (Bahdanau et al., 2014; Vaswani et al., 2017).

One of the common characteristics of these existing models is to model only single reading processing and generate a sequence of hidden states h_t, as a function of the previous hidden states h_{t-1} and the current input (Sutskever et al., 2014; Karpathy et al., 2015). However, the fact is that when we read a text only once, we may merely know the general idea of it, especially when the text is long and obscure. More often than not, we know that fast repeated reading is more effective than slow careful reading, so, for the obscure text, our primary school teacher always teaches us to read several times to get the theme of the text. In addition, this kind of rereading can help us find some of the details that are ignored when we first glance.

In this paper, we propose a novel multi-glance mechanism to model our reading habit: when reading a text, first we will glance through it to get the general meaning and then based on the information we obtained, we will read the text again in order to find some important contents. Based on the multi-glance mechanism we proposed (Fig.1), we design different models for processing the obtained information by the last glance, that it,

27

Proceedings of the Eighth Workshop on Cognitive Aspects of Computational Language Learning and Processing, pages 27–35
Melbourne, Australia, July 19, 2018. ©2018 Association for Computational Linguistics

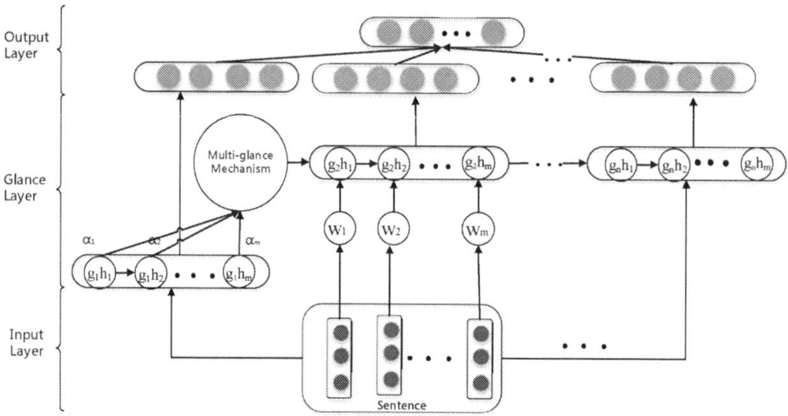

Figure 1: The architecture of Multi-glance Mechanism (MGM) model

Glance Cell Model (GCM) and Glance Gate Model (GGM). GCM has a special cell to memorize the first impression information obtained after finishing the first reading. GGM has a special gate to control current input and output in order to filter words that are not important. The main contributions of this work are summarized as follows:

- We propose a novel multi-glance mechanism which models the habit of reading. Comparing to traditional sequential models, our proposed models can better simulate people's reading process and better understand the content.

- Based on multi-glance mechanism, we propose GCM which can takes the first impression information into consideration. Glance cell model has a special cell to memorize the global impression information we obtain and add it into the current calculation.

- Based on multi-glance mechanism, we propose GGM which adopts a extra gate to ignore the less important words and focus on details in the contents.

2   Related Work

Recurrent neural network has achieved great success because of its effective capability to capture the sequential information. The RNN handles the variable-length sequence by having a recurrent hidden state whose activation at each time step is dependent on that of the previous time. To reduce the negative impact of gradient vanishing, a long short-term memory unit (Hochreiter and Schmidhuber, 1997), which has a more sophisticated activation function, was proposed. Bidi-

rectional recurrent neural networks (Schuster and Paliwal, 1997), e.g bidirectional LSTM networks (Augenstein et al., 2016), combine forward features as well as reverse features of the text. Bidirectional networks, which get the forward features and the reverse features separately, are different from our multi-glance mechanism. A Gated Recurrent Unit (GRU) (Cho et al., 2014) is a good extension of a LSTM unit, because GRU maintains the performance and makes the structure to be simpler. Comparing to a LSTM unit, a GRU has only two gates, an update gate and a reset gate, so it will be faster to train a GRU than a LSTM unit. Attention mechanism (Bahdanau et al., 2014) is used to learn weights for every input, so it can reduce the impact of information redundancy. Now, attention mechanism is commonly used in various models.

3   Methods

In this section, we will introduce the proposed multi-glance mechanism models in detail. We first describe the basic framework of multi-glance mechanism. Afterwards, based on multi-glance mechanism, we describe two glance models, glance cell model and glance gate model.

3.1   Multi-glance Mechanism Model

When reading or analyzing a text, we may read it several times rather than once if we couldn't fully understand its meaning. To model our reading habit, we propose the multi-glance mechanism. The core architecture of the proposed model is shown in Fig.1.

In the following paper, we will describe how the models work when processing a text. Given a training text T, in order to better analyze it, we will read T many times. As shown in Fig. 1, n is the times we will read the text.

For the sake of convenience, we give an example of the 2-glance process here.

First, we glance through the text to capture a general meaning. We use the recurrent network to read the embedding of each word and calculate the hidden states $\{g_1h_1, g_1h_2, \cdots, g_1h_m\}$, where m is the length of the text T. After finishing reading it, we have an impression on the text T. Next, with the guidance of the impression, we give these hidden states weight parameters and feed them into the glance model to continue to read the text for the second time. As we can see, if we read the text only once and don't adopt multi-glance mechanism, this model can be simplified as traditional attention based recurrent model.

At the second time of reading, in view of the general idea of the content we have got, we may ignore the less interesting words and focus on some details in the text. So we utilize a novel glance recurrent model to read embedding $T = \{w_1, w_2, \cdots, w_m\}$ again and calculate the output state $\{g_2h_1, g_2h_2, \cdots, g_2h_m\}$. Based on multi-glance mechanism, we propose two glance recurrent models: that is, **Glance Cell Model**(GCM) and **Glance Gate Model**(GGM).

Comparing to basic recurrent model, glance cell model has a special cell to memorize the general meaning calculated after finishing the first time of reading. Besides, glance gate model has a binary gate to filter the less important words. We describe how two glance recurrent models operate in section 3.2 and section 3.3. Fig.1 gives the main process of the multi-glance mechanism.

3.2 Glance Cell Model

Based on multi-glance mechanism, we propose the glance cell model (GCM). After we finish reading the text T for the first time, we know any of the general meaning of it. This means we have some first impression information about the text. As shown in Fig.2, comparing to the traditional recurrent network, the GCM has a special cell to keep the first impression information. LSTM has been widely adopted for text processing, so we use LSTM to calculate the hidden states g_1h_i.

Thus the glance cell state gc_t^c can be calculated from the weighted sum of hidden states

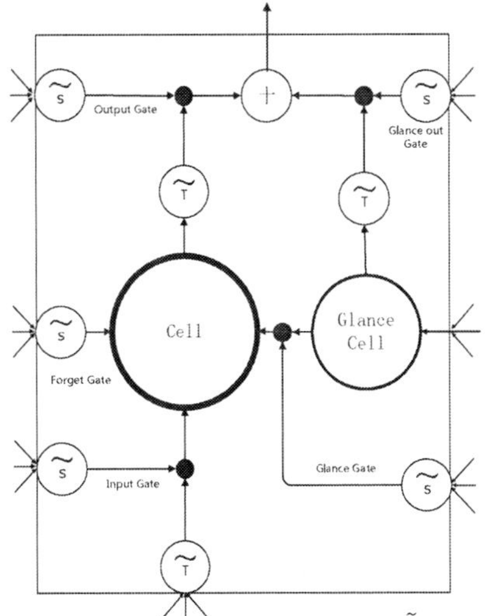

Figure 2: The block of GCM, where $\tilde{T}$ stands for $tanh()$ and $\tilde{S}$ stands for $sigmoid()$.

$\{g_1h_1, g_1h_2, \cdots, g_1h_m\}$:

$$gc_t^c = \sum_{i=1}^{m} \alpha_i \cdot g_1h_i \qquad (1)$$

where α_i measures the impression of i_{th} word for the current glance cell state gc_t^c. Because GCM is a recurrent network as well, the current glance cell state gc_t^c is also influenced by the previous state $g_2h_{t-1}^c$ and the current input w_t. Thus the impression α_i can be defined as:

$$\alpha_i = \frac{exp(f(g_2h_{t-1}^c, w_t, g_1h_i^{lstm}))}{\sum_{i=1}^{m} exp(f(g_2h_{t-1}^c, w_t, g_1h_i^{lstm}))} \qquad (2)$$

where f is the impression function and it can be defined as:

$$f(g_2h_{t-1}^c, w_t, g_1h_i^{lstm}) = gw_c^T \cdot \tanh(W_g^c \cdot [g_2h_{t-1}^c, w_t, g_1h_i^{lstm}] + b^c) \qquad (3)$$

where W_g^c is the weight matrices and gw_c^T is the weight vector.

Besides, glance cell is used to memorize the prior knowledge, we also have a cell, at the second time reading in multi-glance mechanism, to read the text. We use three gates to update and output the cells states, and they can be defined as:

$$i_t^c = \sigma(W_i^c \cdot [g_2h_{t-1}^c, w_t] + b_i^c) \qquad (4)$$

$$f_t^c = \sigma(W_f^c \cdot [g_2h_{t-1}^c, w_t] + b_f^c) \qquad (5)$$

$$o_t^c = \sigma(W_o^c \cdot [g_2h_{t-1}^c, w_t] + b_o^c) \qquad (6)$$

$$\tilde{c}_t^c = \tanh(W_c^c \cdot [g_2h_{t-1}^c, w_t] + b_c^c) \qquad (7)$$

where i_t^c, f_t^c and o_t^c are the gates states, $\sigma()$ is the sigmoid function and $\tilde{c}_t^c$ stands for the input state.

In GCM, in order to adopt the first impression knowledge in the current cell state calculation and output the glance cell state, we use glance input gate and output gate to connect the glance cell and the cell state. The two gates can be defined as:

$$gi_t^c = \sigma(W_{gi}^c \cdot [g_2h_{t-1}^c, w_t, gc_t^c] + b_{gi}^c) \quad (8)$$
$$go_t^c = \sigma(W_{go}^c \cdot [g_2h_{t-1}^c, w_t, gc_t^c] + b_{go}^c) \quad (9)$$

where gi_t^c and go_t^c are the gate states. Thus the cell state can be calculated as:

$$c_t^c = f_t^c \odot c_{t-1}^c + i_t^c \odot \tilde{c}_t^c + gi_t^c \odot gc_t^c \quad (10)$$

where $\odot$ stands for element-wise multiplication.

According to the function, when we read the text at the second time, the current cell state c_t^c contains the previous cell state c_{t-1}^c, current input state $\tilde{c}_t^c$ and the current glance cell state gc_t^c, which is different from the existing recurrent models.

In view of two cells in GCM, the final output of a single block can be calculated as:

$$g_2h_t^c = o_t^c \odot \tanh(c_t^c) + go_t^c \odot \tanh(gc_t^c) \quad (11)$$

We feed the text $T = \{w_1, w_2, \cdots, w_m\}$ embedding into the glance cell model and then obtain the output hidden states $g_2h^c = \{g_2h_1^c, g_2h_2^c, \cdots, g_2h_m^c\}$.

3.3 Glance Gate Model

Based on multi-glance mechanism, we also propose the Glance Gate Model (GGM). The main block of GGM is shown in Fig.3. When we read the text at the second time, in view of the first impression information we obtained, our habit is to ignore the less interesting words directly rather than still reading them again. However, existing RNN models, e.g. LSTM model, have an input gate to control the current input, it still can't set less interesting or important information to zero.

In GGM, we use a binary glance gate to control the input, and it is defined as:

$$gate_t = softmax(W_g^g \cdot [gg_t^g, w_t, g_2h_{t-1}^g] + b^g) \quad (12)$$

where W_g^g is the projection matrix, and softmax only output two states $\{0, 1\}$. In glance gate model (GGM), gg_t^g still models the impression of the text, and calculated by the weighted sum of hidden states $\{g_1h_1, g_1h_2, \cdots, g_1h_m\}$:

$$gg_t^g = \sum_{i=1}^m \beta_i \cdot h_i \quad (13)$$

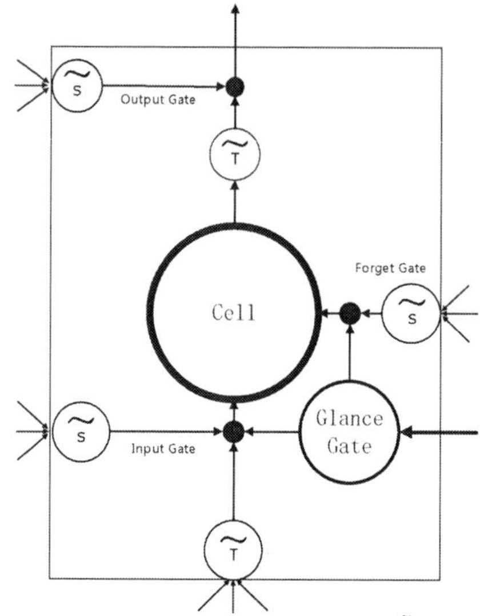

Figure 3: The block of GGM, where $\tilde{T}$ stands for $tanh()$ and $\tilde{S}$ stands for $sigmoid()$.

Where β_i measures the impression of i_{th} word for the current glance gate cell state gg_t^g. For brevity, we will not repeat the function of impression weight β_i and impression function f here.

As shown in the Fig.4, here we give an example of the GGM to process a sentence. Comparing to the LSTM model's input gate, the glance gate only has two states $\{0, 1\}$. When we care about the current word w_i, we input the word w_i into the GGM and update the hidden state. If the current word is meaningless, the GGM will directly discard the input word and keep the previous state without updating the hidden state. Thus the gates, cells states and output hidden states are defined as follows:

$$i_t^g = \sigma(W_i^g \cdot [g_2h_{t-1}^g, w_t] + b_i^g) \odot gate_t \quad (14)$$
$$f_t^g = \sigma(W_f^g \cdot [g_2h_{t-1}^g, w_t] + b_f^g) \odot gate_t \oplus (1 - gate_t) \quad (15)$$
$$o_t^g = \sigma(W_o^g \cdot [g_2h_{t-1}^g, w_t] + b_o^g) \odot gate_t \quad (16)$$
$$\tilde{c}_t^g = \tanh(W_c^g \cdot [g_2h_{t-1}, w_t] + b_c^g) \quad (17)$$
$$c_t^g = f_t^g \odot c_{t-1}^g + i_t^g \odot \tilde{c}_t^g \quad (18)$$
$$g_2h_t^g = o_t^g \odot \tanh(c_t^g) \odot gate_t + g_2h_{t-1}^g \odot (1 - gate_t) \quad (19)$$

where $\oplus$ stands for the element-wise addition.

Note that when the GGM close the glance gate, gate=$\{0\}$, the formulations above can be transformed as:

$$i_t^g = 0 \qquad f_t^g = 1 \qquad o_t^g = 0$$
$$c_t^g = f_t^g \odot c_{t-1}^g + i_t^g \odot \tilde{c}_t^g = c_{t-1}^g$$
$$g_2h_t^g = o_t^g \odot \tanh(c_t^g) \odot gate_t + g_2h_{t-1}^g \odot (1 - gate_t)$$
$$= g_2h_{t-1}^g$$

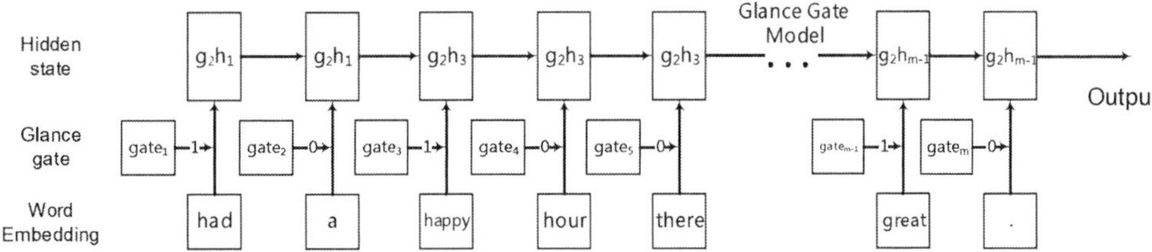

Figure 4: An example of the proposed GGM to process a sentence. In this example, when the glance gate open, the current word will input into the GGM, then output the hidden state. When the glance gate close, the model will ignore the current inputted word and keep the previous hidden state.

so when the glance gate close, the GGM will keep the previous state unchanged. Besides, when the GGM open the glance gate, namely gate=$\{1\}$, the formulations above can be transformed as:

$$i_t^g = \sigma(W_i^g \cdot [g_2 h_{t-1}^g, w_t] + b_i^g)$$
$$f_t^g = \sigma(W_f^g \cdot [g_2 h_{t-1}^g, w_t] + b_f^g)$$
$$o_t^g = \sigma(W_o^g \cdot [g_2 h_{t-1}^g, w_t] + b_o^g)$$
$$c_t^g = f_t^g \odot c_{t-1}^g + i_t \odot \tilde{c}_t^g$$
$$g_2 h_t^g = o_t^g \odot \tanh(c_t^g)$$

So the model can obtain the current input state $\tilde{c}_t^g$ and update the cell state c_t^g. We feed the text T into the GGM and obtain the output hidden states $g_2 h^g = \{g_2 h_1^g, g_2 h_2^g, \cdots, g_2 h_m^g\}$.

3.4 Model Training

To train our multi-glance mechanism models, we adopt softmax layer to project the text representation into the target space of C classes:

$$y = softmax(\tanh(W_s \cdot [\hat{g_2 h}, \hat{g_1 h}] + b_s)) \quad (20)$$

where $\hat{g_2 h}$ is the attention weighted sum of the glance hidden states $\{g_2 h_1, g_2 h_2, \cdots, g_2 h_m\}$, $\hat{g_1 h}$ is the attention weighted sum of the hidden states $\{g_1 h_1, g_1 h_2, \cdots, g_1 h_m\}$.

We use the cross-entropy as training loss:

$$L = -\sum_i \hat{y}_i \cdot \log(y_i) + \alpha|\theta|_2 \quad (21)$$

where $\hat{y}_i$ is the gold distribution for text i, θ represents all the parameters in the model.

4 Experiment

In this section, we conduct experiments on different datasets to evaluate the performance of multi-glance mechanism. We also visualize the glance layers in both glance models.

4.1 Datasets and Experimental Setting

We evaluate the effectiveness of our glance models on four different datasets . Yelp 2013 and Yelp2014 are obtained from the Yelp Dataset Challenge. IMDB dataset was built by Tang et al. (2015). Amazon reviews are obtained from A-mazon Fine Food reviews. The statistics of the datasets are summarized in Table 1.

datasets	rank	docs	$\frac{sens}{docs}$	vocs
IMDB	1-10	84,919	16.08	105373
Amazon	1-5	556,770	5.67	119870
Yelp2013	1-5	78,966	10.89	48957
Yelp2014	1-5	231,163	11.41	93197

Table 1: Statistical information of IMDB, Amazon, Yelp 2013, Yelp 2014 datasets

The datasets are split into training, validation and test sets with the proportion of 8:1:1. We use the Stanford CoreNLP for tokenization and sentence splitting. For training, we pre-train the word vector and set the dimension to be 200 with Skip-Gram (Mikolov et al., 2013). In our glance models, the dimensions of hidden states and cells states are set to 200 and the hidden states and cells states initialized randomly. We adopt AdaDelta (Zeiler, 2012) to train our models , select the best configuration based on the validation set, and evaluate the performance on the test set.

4.2 Baselines

We compare our glance models with the following baseline methods.

Trigram adopts unigrams, bigrams and trigrams as text features and trains a SVM classifier.
TextFeature adopts more abundant features including n-grams, lexicon features, etc, and

Models \ Datasets	IMDB	Yelp2014	Yelp2013	Amazon
Trigram	39.9	57.7	56.9	54.3
TextFeature	40.2	57.2	55.6	-
PVDM	34.1	56.4	55.4	-
RNTN+RNN	40.0	58.2	57.4	-
NSC	42.7	62.7	62.2	75.1
RNN+ATT	43.1	63.2	62.7	75.4
GGM	43.7	63.4	63.0	75.2
GCM	**44.2**	**64.2**	**63.6**	**76.7**

Table 2: Text analysis results on IMDB, Yelp2014, yelp2013 and Amazon datasets. Evaluation metrics is Accuracy in percentage (higher the better). The best performance in each group is in **bold.**

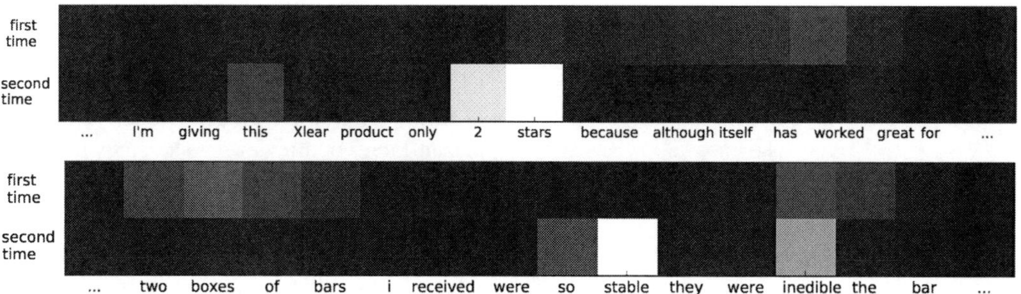

Figure 5: Visualization of the weights when we read the text twice with glance cell model (whiter color means higher weight).

trains a SVM classifier. (Kiritchenko et al., 2014)

RNTN+RNN uses Recursive Neural Neural Tensor Network to represent the sentences and Recurrent Neural Network to document analysis. (Socher et al., 2013)

PVDM leverages Paragraph Vector Distributed Memory (PVDM) algorithm for document classification.(Le and Mikolov, 2014)

NSC regards the text as a sequence and uses max or average pooling of the hidden states as features for classification.(Chen et al., 2016)

RNN+ATT adopts attention mechanism to select the important hidden states and represents the text as a weight sum of hidden states.

4.3 Model Comparisons

The experimental results are shown in Table 2. We can see that multi-glance mechanism based models, glance gate model (GGM) and glance cell model (GCM), achieve a better accuracy than traditional recurrent models, because of the guidance of the overview meaning we obtain at the first time of reading. With that guidance, we will get a better understanding of the text. While comparing to our glance models, existing RNN models read the text only once so they cannot have the general meaning to help them understand the text.

Comparing to attention-based recurrent models, the proposed glance cell model still has a better performance. The main reason for this is that when we read the text with the multi-glance mechanism, the glance hidden states have a better understanding of the text, so when we calculate the attention weight on each hidden states, the final output will also be better to represent the text.

When comparing the models we proposed, glance cell model gives a better performance than glance gate model. This is because we use multi-glance mechanism to filter words in glance gate model while we use multi-glance mechanism to add general information in glance cell model. Even though we only ignore the less important words in glance gate model when the gate is closed, some information is still lost comparing to glance cell model.

4.4 Model Analysis for Glance Cell Model

To establish the effectiveness of GCM, we choose some reviews in Amazon dataset and visualize them in the Fig.5. In each sub-figure, the first line

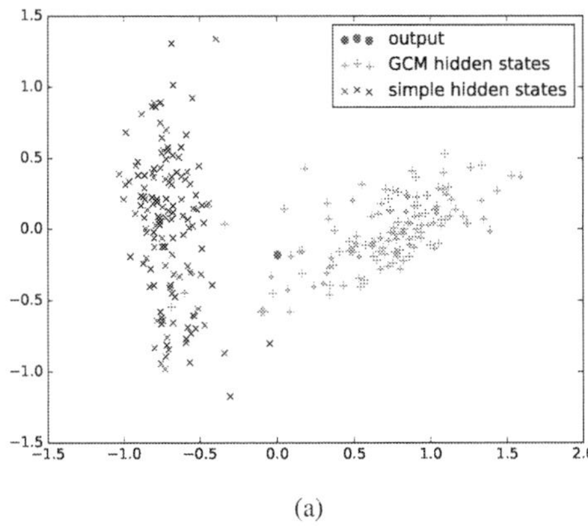
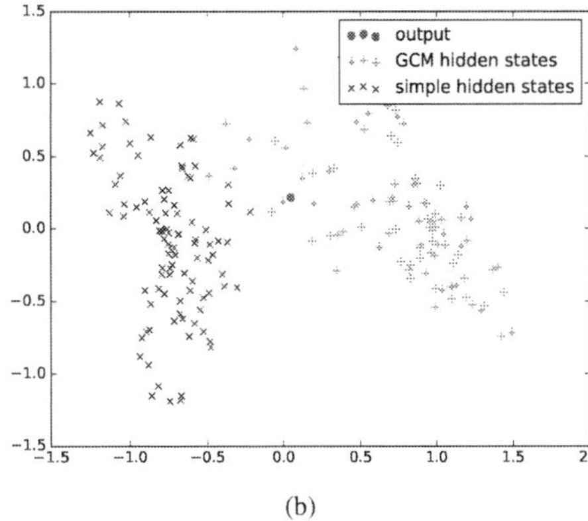

(a)   (b)

Figure 6: Visualization of the hidden states calculated by simple RNN model $\{g_1h_1, g_1h_2, \cdots, g_1h_t\}$ (the purple spots), Glance Cell Model $\{g_2h_1^c, g_2h_2^c, \cdots, g_2h_t^c\}$ (the blue spots) and the final text representation (the red spots).

Figure 7: Visualization of the gate state in Glance Gate Model. The words in color (blue and red) are input into the GGM, that meas the gate state is open. The words in gray are ignored by the GGM.

is the visualization of the weights when we read the text at the first time, the second line is the visualization that we read at the second time. Note that, whiter color means higher weight.

As shown in Fig.5, the first review has wrote the ranking stars in the text, which is a determining factor in product reviews, but we ignore them when we read at the first time. Well, with the guidance of multi-glance mechanism, when we read them again, we can not only find the ranking stars, but also give them high weights.

In the second review, comparing the results we read at the first time and the second time, though we may focus on some of the same words, e.g. inedible, we will give them different weights. We can observe that when reading at the second time, we give word 'inedible' a higher weight and word 'the' a lower the weight. The glance cell model can increase the weights of important words, so we can focus on more useful words when using multi-glance mechanism and glance cell model.

Next, we also choose two reviews in the dataset and visualize the hidden states which calculated by the glance cell model and a traditional recurrent model. As aforementioned in this paper, when using multi-glance mechanism, we will get the local information comparing to simple RNN models. As shown in Fig.6, the purple spots and the blue spots are the visualizations of the hidden states, and the purple spots belong to the simple RNN model while the blue spots belong to the glance cell model. The spot in red is the visualization of the final text representation. Note that, we use PCA to reduce the dimensions of the hidden states here. We can see that the blue spots are much more closer to the red spots than the purple spots, which mean the glance cell hidden states are more closer to the final text representations. It is the local information that makes the difference. So we can obtain a more general idea when using the glance cell model we proposed.

4.5 Model Analysis for Glance Gate Model

To demonstrate the effectiveness of the glance gate model, we choose a review in IMDB dataset and visualize the values of gates. As mentioned in this paper, the gates only have two states, closed and open. As shown in Fig. 7, the words in gray mean

33

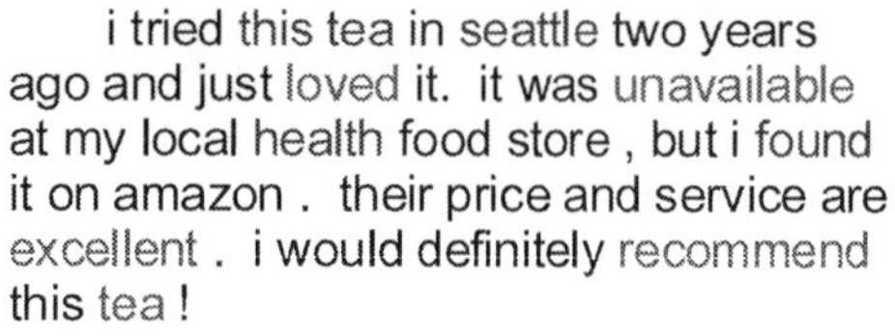

(a) Model with Multi-glance Mechanism

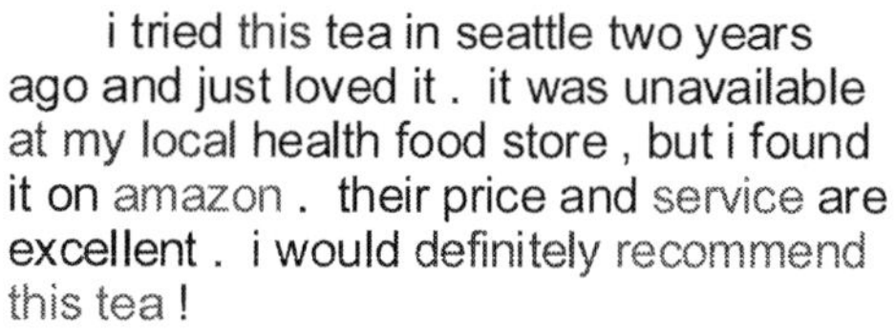

(b) Simple RNN with Attention Mechanism

Figure 9: Visualization of the multi-glance mechanism weights and the simple RNN attention mechanism weights.

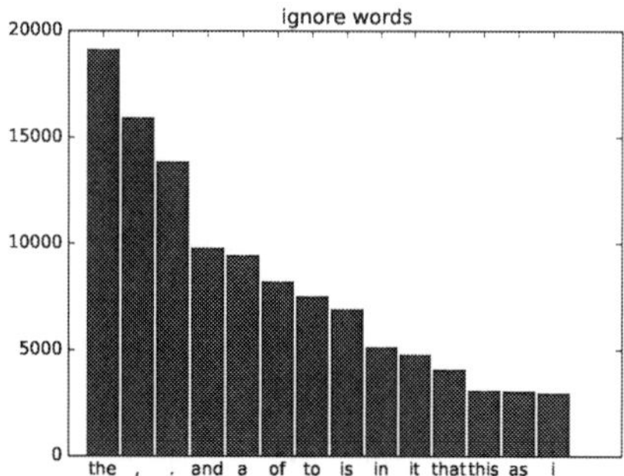

Figure 8: The statistics of the Top-ignored words in 1000 IMDB reviews.

when we read these words, the gates in GGM are closed. So these words are unable to pass through the gate. These words in color (blue and red) mean that the gates are open when we read these words. We can observe that when we read the text again, the glance gate model can ignore the less important words and focus on the more useful words. Surprisingly, the most important words are found, e.g. enjoyable, best comedies and funny (the red words in Fig.7). The model is able to find the adjectives, verbs and some nouns, which is more useful in the text understanding.

Besides, we also count the top-ignored words in 1000 IMDB reviews, and the results are shown in the Fig.8. We can see that most of the prepositions and adverds are ignored. Thus glance gate model can filter the less important words and concentrate on the more informative words.

4.6 Comparing to RNN with Attention Mechanism

To demonstrate the effectiveness of the multi-glance mechanism, we choose a review in Amazon dataset and visualize the parameters of weights in multi-glance model and attention based RNN model. As shown in Fig.9, the words in color (red and blue) are the top 10 important words in the review the word in red color are the top 5 important

words. We can observe that multi-glance mechanism can find the more useful words, e.g. loved, excellent. What's more, multi-glance mechansim also can give these important words higher weights comparing to simple attention based RNN models which only read the review once.

5 Conclusion and Future work

In this paper, we propose a multi-glance mechanism in order to model the habit of reading. When we read a text, we may read it several times rather than once in order to gain a better understanding. Usually, we first read the text quickly and get a general idea. Under the guidance of this first impression, we will read many times until we get enough information we need. What's more, based on the multi-glance mechanism, we also propose two glance models, glance cell model and glance gate model. The glance cell model has a special cell to memorize the first impression information we obtain and add it into the current calculation. The glance gate model adopts a special gate to ignore the less important words when we read the text at the second time with multi-glance mechanism. The experimental results show that when we use the multi-glance mechanism to read the text, we are able to get a better understanding of the text. Besides, the glance cell model can memorise the first impression information and the glance gate model is able to filter the less important words, e.g. the, of. We will continue our work as follows:

- How to construct the first impression information more effectively? As proposed in this paper, some of the words in the text are redundant for us to understand text. So, we will sample some words of the text when reading it at the first time.

- The next step will be taken in the direction of algorithm acceleration and model lightweight design.

Acknowledgments

This work was supported in part by the Research Fund for the development of strategic emerging industries by ShenZhen city (No.JCYJ20160331104524983 and No.JCYJ20170412170118573).

References

Isabelle Augenstein, Tim Rockt?schel, Andreas Vlachos, and Kalina Bontcheva. 2016. Stance detection with bidirectional conditional encoding. pages 876–885.

Dzmitry Bahdanau, Kyunghyun Cho, and Yoshua Bengio. 2014. Neural machine translation by jointly learning to align and translate. *arXiv preprint arXiv:1409.0473*.

Huimin Chen, Maosong Sun, Cunchao Tu, Yankai Lin, and Zhiyuan Liu. 2016. Neural sentiment classification with user and product attention. In *Proceedings of the 2016 Conference on Empirical Methods in Natural Language Processing*, pages 1650–1659.

Kyunghyun Cho, Bart Van Merriënboer, Caglar Gulcehre, Dzmitry Bahdanau, Fethi Bougares, Holger Schwenk, and Yoshua Bengio. 2014. Learning phrase representations using rnn encoder-decoder for statistical machine translation. *arXiv preprint arXiv:1406.1078*.

Junyoung Chung, Caglar Gulcehre, KyungHyun Cho, and Yoshua Bengio. 2014. Empirical evaluation of gated recurrent neural networks on sequence modeling. *arXiv preprint arXiv:1412.3555*.

Bhuwan Dhingra, Hanxiao Liu, Zhilin Yang, William W Cohen, and Ruslan Salakhutdinov. 2016. Gated-attention readers for text comprehension. *arXiv preprint arXiv:1606.01549*.

Sepp Hochreiter and Jürgen Schmidhuber. 1997. Long short-term memory. *Neural Computation*, 9(8):1735–1780.

Andrej Karpathy, Justin Johnson, and Li Fei-Fei. 2015. Visualizing and understanding recurrent networks. *arXiv preprint arXiv:1506.02078*.

Yoon Kim. 2014. Convolutional neural networks for sentence classification. *arXiv preprint arXiv:1408.5882*.

Svetlana Kiritchenko, Xiaodan Zhu, and Saif M Mohammad. 2014. Sentiment analysis of short informal texts. *Journal of Artificial Intelligence Research*, 50:723–762.

Quoc Le and Tomas Mikolov. 2014. Distributed representations of sentences and documents. In *International Conference on Machine Learning*, pages 1188–1196.

Tomas Mikolov, Kai Chen, Greg Corrado, and Jeffrey Dean. 2013. Efficient estimation of word representations in vector space. *arXiv preprint arXiv:1301.3781*.

Mike Schuster and Kuldip K Paliwal. 1997. Bidirectional recurrent neural networks. *IEEE Transactions on Signal Processing*, 45(11):2673–2681.

Richard Socher, Alex Perelygin, Jean Wu, Jason Chuang, Christopher D Manning, Andrew Ng, and Christopher Potts. 2013. Recursive deep models for semantic compositionality over a sentiment treebank. In *Proceedings of the 2013 conference on empirical methods in natural language processing*, pages 1631–1642.

Ilya Sutskever, Oriol Vinyals, and Quoc V Le. 2014. Sequence to sequence learning with neural networks. In *Advances in neural information processing systems*, pages 3104–3112.

Kai Sheng Tai, Richard Socher, and Christopher D. Manning. 2015. Improved semantic representations from tree-structured long short-term memory networks. In *Proceedings of the 53rd Annual Meeting of the Association for Computational Linguistics*, pages 1556–1566.

Duyu Tang, Bing Qin, and Ting Liu. 2015. Document modeling with gated recurrent neural network for sentiment classification. In *Proceedings of the 2015 conference on empirical methods in natural language processing*, pages 1422–1432.

Duyu Tang, Furu Wei, Nan Yang, Ming Zhou, Ting Liu, and Bing Qin. 2014. Learning sentiment-specific word embedding for twitter sentiment classification. In *Proceedings of the 52nd Annual Meeting of the Association for Computational Linguistics (Volume 1: Long Papers)*, volume 1, pages 1555–1565.

Ashish Vaswani, Noam Shazeer, Niki Parmar, Jakob Uszkoreit, Llion Jones, Aidan N Gomez, Łukasz Kaiser, and Illia Polosukhin. 2017. Attention is all you need. In *Advances in Neural Information Processing Systems*, pages 6000–6010.

Zichao Yang, Diyi Yang, Chris Dyer, Xiaodong He, Alex Smola, and Eduard Hovy. 2016. Hierarchical attention networks for document classification. In *Proceedings of the 2016 Conference of the North American Chapter of the Association for Computational Linguistics: Human Language Technologies*, pages 1480–1489.

Matthew D Zeiler. 2012. Adadelta: an adaptive learning rate method. *arXiv preprint arXiv:1212.5701*.

Xiang Zhang, Junbo Zhao, and Yann LeCun. 2015. Character-level convolutional networks for text classification. In *Advances in neural information processing systems*, pages 649–657.

Predicting Japanese Word Order in Double Object Constructions

Masayuki Asahara

National Institute for Japanese
Language and Linguistics, Japan
Center for Corpus Development

masayu-a@ninjal.ac.jp

Satoshi Nambu

Monash University, Australia
School of Languages, Literatures,
Cultures and Linguistics

satoshi.nambu@monash.edu

Shin-Ichiro Sano

Keio University, Japan
Faculty of Business and Commerce

s-sano@keio.jp

Abstract

This paper presents a statistical model to predict Japanese word order in the double object constructions. We employed a Bayesian linear mixed model with manually annotated predicate-argument structure data. The findings from the refined corpus analysis confirmed the effects of information status of an NP as 'given-new ordering' in addition to the effects of 'long-before-short' as a tendency of the general Japanese word order.

1 Introduction

Because Japanese exhibits a flexible word order, potential factors that predict word orders of a given construction in Japanese have been recently delved into, particularly in the field of computational linguistics (Yamashita and Kondo, 2011; Orita, 2017). One of the major findings relevant to the current study is 'long-before-short', whereby a long noun phrase (NP) tends to be scrambled ahead of a short NP (Yamashita and Chang, 2001).

This paper sheds light on those factors in double object constructions (DOC), where either (1) an indirect object (IOBJ) or (2) a direct object (DOBJ) can precede the other object:

(1) Taro-ga Hanako-ni hon-o ageta.
  Taro-SBJ Hanako-IOBJ book-DOBJ gave
  'Taro gave Hanako a book.'

(2) Taro-ga hon-o Hanako-ni ageta.
  Taro-SBJ book-DOBJ Hanako-IOBJ gave
  'Taro gave Hanako a book.'

Since both of the word orders are available, studies in theoretical syntax have been disputing about what is the canonical word order under the hypothesis of deriving one word order (i.e., either IOBJ-DOBJ or DOBJ-IOBJ) from another in the context of derivational syntax (Hoji, 1985; Miyagawa, 1997; Matsuoka, 2003). In this paper, we do not attempt to adjudicate upon the dispute solely based on the frequency of the two word orders in a corpus, but aim to detect principal factors that predict the word order in the DOC, which may eventually lead to resolving the issue in theoretical syntax. To that end, we employed a Bayesian linear mixed model with potential factors affecting the word orders as a preliminary study.

Other than the factor 'long-before-short' proposed in previous studies, the key factor in the current study is an information status of an NP in a given context under the theoretical framework of information structure (Lambrecht, 1994; Vallduví and Engdahl, 1996). The framework provides us key categories, such as (informationally) given/old, new, topic, and focus, to classify an NP as how it functions in a particular context. We assume the information status as one of the principle predictors based on the following two reasons; (i) a discourse-given element tends to precede a discourse-new one in a sentence in Japanese (Kuno, 1978, 2004; Nakagawa, 2016), (ii) focused or new elements in Japanese tend to appear in a position immediately preceding the predicate (Kuno, 1978; Kim, 1988; Ishihara, 2001; Vermeulen, 2012). These two claims regarding the general word order of Japanese are combined into the following hypothesis regarding the word orders in the DOC.

(3) Our hypothesis:
  In the DOC, a discourse-given object tends to appear on the left of the other object, and a discourse-new object tends to be on the right side.

Incorporating the information status of an NP with another factor 'long-before-short' proposed in the previous studies, we built a statistical model

Proceedings of the Eighth Workshop on Cognitive Aspects of Computational Language Learning and Processing, pages 36–40
Melbourne, Australia, July 19, 2018. ©2018 Association for Computational Linguistics

Table 1: Comparison with Preceding Work

	(Sasano and Okumura, 2016)	(Orita, 2017)	The current work
corpus	Web Corpus	NAIST Text Corpus	BCCWJ-PAS and BCCWJ-DepPara
genres	Web	Newspaper	Newspaper, Books, Magazines, Yahoo! Answes, Blog, Whitepaper
target	SUBJ-IOBJ-DOBJ-PRED	SUBJ-DOBJ-PRED	SUBJ-IOBJ-DOBJ-PRED
documents	n/a	2,929	1,980
sentences	around 10 billion	38,384	57,225
tuples	648 types × 350,000 samples	3,103 tokens	584 tokens
features	verb types	syntactic priming, NP length, given-new, and animacy	NP length, and given-new
analysis	linear regression and NPMI	logistic regression (glm)	Bayesian linear mixed model (rstan)

to predict the word orders in the DOC. One important advantage of our study is that, with the latest version of the corpus we used (See Section 3), the information status of an NP can be analyzed not simply by bipartite groups as either pronoun (given) or others (new) but by the number of co-indexed items in a preceding text.

2 Preceding Work

Table 1 shows a comparison with the latest corpus studies on Japanese word ordering.

Sasano and Okumura (2016) explored the canonical word order of Japanese double object constructions (either SUBJ-IOBJ-DOBJ-PRED or SUBJ-DOBJ-IOBJ-PRED) by a large-scale web corpus. The web corpus contains 10 billion sentences parsed by the Japanese morphological analyzer JUMAN and the syntactic analyzer KNP. In their analysis, the parse trees without syntactic ambiguity were extracted from the web corpus, and the word order was estimated by verb types with a linear regression and normalized pointwise mutual information. Their model did not include any inter-sentential factors such as coreference.

Orita (2017) made a statistical model to predict a scrambled word order as (direct) object-subject. She used the NAIST Text corpus which has a manual annotation of predicate-argument structure and coreference information. She explored the effect of syntactic priming, NP length, animacy, and given-new bipartite information status (given was defined as having a lexically identical item in a previous text). Her frequentism statistical analysis (simple logistic regression) did not detect a significant effect of the given-new factor on the order of a subject and an object.

As a preliminary study which features coreferential information as a potential factor, we used manual annotation of syntactic dependencies, predicate-argument structures and coreference information, employing a Bayesian statistical analysis on the small-sized well-maintained data.

3 Experiments

3.1 Corpora: BCCWJ-PAS

We used the 'Balanced Corpus of Contemporary Written Japanese' (BCCWJ) (Maekawa et al., 2014), which includes morphological information and sentence boundaries, as the target corpus. The corpus was extended with annotations of predicate-argument structures as BCCWJ-PAS (BCCWJ Predicate Argument Structures), based on the NAIST Text Corpus (Iida et al., 2007) compatible standard. We revised all annotations of the BCCWJ-PAS data, including subjects (with case marker -*ga*), direct objects (with case marker -*o*), and indirect objects (with case marker -*ni*), as well as coreferential information of NPs. After the revision process, syntactic dependencies of BCCWJ-DepPara (Asahara and Matsumoto, 2016) were overlaid on the predicate-argument structures.

We extracted 4-tuples of subject (subj), direct object (dobj), indirect object (iobj) and predicate (pred) from the overlaid data. Excluding 4-tuples with zero-pronoun, case alternation, or inter-clause dependencies from the target data, we obtained 584 samples of the 4-tuples.

Figure 1 shows an example sentence from BCCWJ Yahoo! Answer sample (OC09_04653). The surface is segmented into base phrases, which is the unit to evaluate the distance between two constituents as in the following pairs of the 4-tuples: subj-pred ($\text{dist}^{subj}_{pred}$), dobj-pred ($\text{dist}^{dobj}_{pred}$), iobj-pred ($\text{dist}^{iobj}_{pred}$), subj-iobj ($\text{dist}^{subj}_{iobj}$), subj-dobj ($\text{dist}^{subj}_{dobj}$), and iobj-dobj ($\text{dist}^{iobj}_{dobj}$). The distance was calculated from the rightmost word in each pair. For example, in Figure 1, $\text{dist}^{subj}_{pred}$ is identified as the distance between "" and "" as 4.

Verifying effects of 'long-before-short' as a

Table 2: Basic Statistics

	min	1Q	med	mean	3Q	max
$\text{dist}^{subj}_{pred}$	1.0	4.0	5.0	5.8	7.0	23.0
$\text{dist}^{dobj}_{pred}$	1.0	1.0	1.0	1.7	2.0	13.0
$\text{dist}^{iobj}_{pred}$	1.0	1.0	2.0	2.3	3.0	17.0
$\text{dist}^{subj}_{iobj}$	-14.0	1.0	3.0	3.5	5.0	21.0
$\text{dist}^{subj}_{dobj}$	-10.0	2.0	3.0	4.1	5.0	22.0
$\text{dist}^{iobj}_{dobj}$	-12.0	-1.0	1.0	0.6	2.0	16.0
N^{subj}_{mora}	2.0	4.0	5.0	6.5	8.0	32.0
N^{dobj}_{mora}	2.0	3.0	4.0	5.3	6.0	37.0
N^{iobj}_{mora}	2.0	4.0	5.0	6.1	7.0	52.0
N^{subj}_{coref}	0.0	0.0	1.0	6.9	6.0	105.0
N^{dobj}_{coref}	0.0	0.0	0.0	0.5	0.0	44.0
N^{iobj}_{coref}	0.0	0.0	0.0	3.1	1.0	99.0

general Japanese word-order tendency, lengths of constituents were modeled as fixed effects in the statistical analysis. The lengths of subject, direct object and indirect object were calculated based on a mora count (in pronunciation) available in BCCWJ as N^{subj}_{mora}, N^{dobj}_{mora}, and N^{iobj}_{mora}, respectively. For example, in Figure 1, N^{subj}_{mora} is the number of morae of " " (*sono kanojoga*), which is 6. Note that an NP may contain more than one base phrase including an embedded clause. We evaluated the maximum span of the dependency subtree in BCCWJ-DepPara as a length of the NP.

In addition, the numbers of coreferent items in a preceding text were modeled as fixed effects. The numbers of coreferent items for subject, direct object and indirect object were obtained from the BCCWJ-PAS annotations as N^{subj}_{coref}, N^{dobj}_{coref}, and N^{iobj}_{coref}, respectively. Table 2 shows the basic statistics of the distance, mora, and number of coreferent items.

3.2 Statistical Analysis

We used Bayesian linear mixed models (Sorensen et al., 2016) (BLMM) for the statistical analysis on the distance between arguments as well as an argument and its predicate. We modeled the following formula:

$$\text{dist}^{left}_{right} \sim \text{Normal}(\mu, \sigma)$$

$$\mu \leftarrow \alpha + \beta^{subj}_{mora} \cdot N^{subj}_{mora} + \beta^{subj}_{coref} \cdot N^{subj}_{coref}$$
$$+ \beta^{dobj}_{mora} \cdot N^{dobj}_{mora} + \beta^{dobj}_{coref} \cdot N^{dobj}_{coref}$$
$$+ \beta^{iobj}_{mora} \cdot N^{iobj}_{mora} + \beta^{iobj}_{coref} \cdot N^{iobj}_{coref}.$$

$\text{dist}^{left}_{right}$ (e.g. $\text{dist}^{subj}_{iobj}$: distance between subject (left) and indirect object (right)) stands for the distance between left and right elements, which is

modeled by a normal distribution with average μ and stdev σ. μ is defined by a linear formula with an intercept α and two types of interest coefficients. N^{subj}_{mora}, N^{dobj}_{mora}, and N^{iobj}_{mora} are the number of morae of a subject, a direct object, and an indirect object, respectively. The subject and objects can be composed of more than one phrase, and when they contain a clause, the number of morae was defined with the clause length.

N^{subj}_{coref}, N^{dobj}_{coref}, and N^{iobj}_{coref} stand for the number of preceding coreferent NPs of a subject, a direct object, and an indirect, respectively. β^a_b are the slope parameters for the coefficients N^a_b. Note that the distance was measured by the number of base phrase units, and a minus value indicates a distance in an opposite direction.

We ran 4 chains $\times$ 2000 post-warmup iteration, and all models were converged.

4 Results and Discussions

4.1 Results

Table 3 shows the estimated parameters by the BLMM; the values are means with standard deviations (in brackets). The findings are summarized as follows.

First, the distance between a subject and its predicate ($\text{dist}^{subj}_{pred}$) is affected only by the number of morae of a subject, which indicates that a longer subject NP has a longer distance from its predicate.

Second, the distance between a direct object and its predicate ($\text{dist}^{dobj}_{pred}$) is affected by the number of morae of the direct object, the number of its preceding coreferent items, and the number of morae of the indirect object. It indicates that i) a longer direct object has a longer distance from its predicate, ii) a direct object with more coreferent items in a preceding text has a longer distance from its predicate, and iii) a longer indirect object makes shorter the distance between the direct object and its predicate.

Third, the distance between an indirect object and its predicate ($\text{dist}^{iobj}_{pred}$) is affected by the number of morae of the indirect object, the number of its preceding coreferent items, the number of morae of a direct object, and the number of preceding coreferent items of a subject. It indicates that i) a longer indirect object has a longer distance from its predicate, ii) an indirect object with more coreferent items in a preceding text has a longer distance from its predicate, iii) a longer direct ob-

$$\text{dist}^{subj}_{pred} = 4 \quad \text{dist}^{dobj}_{pred} = 1 \quad \text{dist}^{iobj}_{pred} = 2 \quad \text{dist}^{subj}_{iobj} = 2 \quad \text{dist}^{subj}_{dobj} = 3 \quad \text{dist}^{iobj}_{dobj} = 1$$

surface						
pronunciation	sono	kanojoga	mada	bokuni	keigoo	tsukaimasu
translation	that	she	yet	me	honorific-OBJ	use
predicate-argument	SUBJ			IOBJ	DOBJ	PRED
morae	$N^{subj}_{mora} = 6$			$N^{iobj}_{mora} = 3$	$N^{dobj}_{mora} = 4$	
coreference	$N^{subj}_{coref} = 2$			$N^{iobj}_{coref} = 3$	$N^{dobj}_{coref} = 0$	

Figure 1: Example sentence (BCCWJ Yahoo! Answers:OC09_04653)

Table 3: Evaluation of distances

distance	α	β^{subj}_{mora}	β^{dobj}_{mora}	β^{iobj}_{mora}	β^{subj}_{coref}	β^{dobj}_{coref}	β^{iobj}_{coref}	σ
$\text{dist}^{subj}_{pred}$	4.814***	0.146***	-0.031	0.040	0.002	-0.056	-0.009	3.323
	(0.375)	(0.040)	(0.042)	(0.032)	(0.011)	(0.043)	(0.016)	(0.100)
$\text{dist}^{dobj}_{pred}$	1.593***	-0.009	0.061***	-0.032**	-0.001	0.037**	-0.005	1.072
	(0.128)	(0.013)	(0.014)	(0.011)	(0.004)	(0.014)	(0.005)	(0.032)
$\text{dist}^{iobj}_{pred}$	2.100**	-0.022	-0.056**	0.112***	-0.018***	-0.045	0.037***	1.861
	(0.217)	(0.022)	(0.023)	(0.018)	(0.006)	(0.024)	(0.009)	(0.055)
$\text{dist}^{subj}_{iobj}$	2.668***	0.171***	0.026	0.071**	0.020	-0.011	-0.046**	3.577
	(0.420)	(0.043)	(0.045)	(0.035)	(0.012)	(0.047)	(0.017)	(0.108)
$\text{dist}^{subj}_{dobj}$	3.205***	0.155***	-0.092**	0.072**	0.003	-0.094**	-0.004	3.452
	(0.404)	(0.041)	(0.043)	(0.034)	(0.012)	(0.046)	(0.017)	(0.103)
$\text{dist}^{iobj}_{dobj}$	0.502	-0.013	-0.117***	0.143***	-0.017**	-0.081**	0.041***	2.436
	(0.287)	(0.029)	(0.030)	(0.024)	(0.008)	(0.033)	(0.011)	(0.071)

$** > \pm 2SD, *** > \pm 3SD$

ject makes shorter the distance between the indirect object and its predicate, and iv) a subject with more coreferent items makes shorter the distance between the indirect object and its predicate.

The distance between arguments ($\text{dist}^{subj}_{iobj}$, $\text{dist}^{subj}_{dobj}$, and $\text{dist}^{iobj}_{dobj}$) represents nearly the same tendency as the combination of the predicate-argument distance. However, the number of morae of an argument is correlated with the length of the argument (i.e., the number of base phrases), and thus, the distance between the leftmost and rightmost arguments (e.g. subject, direct object) is affected by the number of morae of the middle argument (e.g. N^{iobj}_{mora}).

4.2 Discussions

The results revealed that the subject tends to precede the direct and indirect objects in the double object constructions. Although the indirect object tends to precede the direct object, it is not significant (p=0.09).

The estimated coefficients for the number of coreferent items (N^{dobj}_{coref} for $\text{dist}^{dobj}_{pred}$ and N^{iobj}_{coref} for $\text{dist}^{iobj}_{pred}$) support our hypothesis in (3) as 'given-new ordering' for the direct and indirect objects. An object with many preceding coreferent items tends to be farther from a corresponding predicate.

The estimated coefficients for the number of morae (N^{subj}_{mora} for $\text{dist}^{subj}_{pred}$, N^{dobj}_{mora} for $\text{dist}^{dobj}_{pred}$ and N^{iobj}_{mora} for $\text{dist}^{iobj}_{pred}$) indicate that the orders of all arguments in the DOC follow 'long-before-short'. It is also confirmed by the minus values as the estimated coefficients for the number of morae of one object in relation to the order of the other object and its predicate (N^{dobj}_{mora} for $\text{dist}^{iobj}_{pred}$ and N^{iobj}_{mora} for $\text{dist}^{dobj}_{pred}$), suggesting that a longer object tends to precede the other object in the DOC.

5   Conclusions

This article presents a Bayesian statistical analysis on Japanese word ordering in the double object constructions. It revealed the 'given-new ordering' for the indirect and direct objects and also confirmed the 'long-before-short' tendency for all of the arguments in the constructions.

Setting off from the current preliminary study, our future work is to investigate effects of verb type and animacy of an NP. We are currently annotating the labels of a Japanese thesaurus 'Word List by Semantic Principles' (WLSP) (Kokuritsukokugokenkyusho, 1964), which enables us to explore those effects.

Acknowledgments

This work was supported by JSPS KAKENHI Grants Numbers JP15K12888 and JP17H00917 and is a project of the Center for Corpus Development, NINJAL.

References

Masayuki Asahara and Yuji Matsumoto. 2016. BCCWJ-DepPara: A Syntactic Annotation Treebank on the 'Balanced Corpus of Contemporary Written Japanese'. In *Proceedings of the 12th Workshop on Asian Language Resources (ALR12)*, pages 49–58, Osaka, Japan. The COLING 2016 Organizing Committee.

Hajime Hoji. 1985. *Logical Form Constraints and Configurational Structures in Japanese*. Ph.D. thesis, University of Washington.

Ryu Iida, Mamoru Komachi, Kentaro Inui, and Yuji Matsumoto. 2007. Annotating a Japanese Text Corpus with Predicate-Argument and Coreference Relations. In *Proceedings of the Linguistic Annotation Workshop*, pages 132–139, Prague, Czech Republic. Association for Computational Linguistics.

Shin-ichiro Ishihara. 2001. Stress, focus, and scrambling in japanese. In Ora Matushansky Elena Guerzoni, editor, *MITWPL 39*, pages 142–175. Cambridge, MA: MITWPL.

Alan Hyun-Oak Kim. 1988. Preverbal focusing and type xxiii languages. In Jessica Wirth Michael Hammond, Edith A. Moravcsik, editor, *Studies in syntactic typology*, pages 147–169. Amsterdam: John Benjamins.

Kokuritsukokugokenkyusho, editor. 1964. *Bunruigoihyo [Word List by Semantic Principles]*. Shuei Shuppan.

Susumu Kuno. 1978. *Danwa no bunpoo [Grammar of discourse]*. Taishukan Shoten, Tokyo.

Susumu Kuno. 2004. Empathy and direct discourse perspectives. In Lawrence Horn and Gregory Ward, editors, *The handbook of pragmatics*, pages 315–343. Oxford: Blackwell.

Knud Lambrecht. 1994. *Information Structure and Sentence Form: Topic, Focus, and the Mental Representations of Discourse Referents*, volume 71 of *Cambridge Studies in Linguistics*. Cambridge University Press.

Kikuo Maekawa, Makoto Yamazaki, Toshinobu Ogiso, Takehiko Maruyama, Hideki Ogura, Wakako Kashino, Hanae Koiso, Masaya Yamaguchi, Makiro Tanaka, and Yasuharu Den. 2014. Balanced Corpus of Contemporary Written Japanese. *Language Resources and Evaluation*, 48:345–371.

Mikinari Matsuoka. 2003. Two types of ditransitive constructions in japanese. *Journal of East Asian Linguistics*, 12:171–203.

Shigeru Miyagawa. 1997. Against optional scrambling. *Linguistic Inquiry*, 28:1–26.

Natsuko Nakagawa. 2016. *Information Structure in Spoken Japanese: Particles, word order, and intonation*. Ph.D. thesis, Kyoto University.

Naho Orita. 2017. Predicting Japanese scrambling in the wild. In *Proceedings of the 7th Workshop on Cognitive Modeling and Computational Linguistics (CMCL 2017)*, pages 41–45, Valencia, Spain. Association for Computational Linguistics.

Ryohei Sasano and Manabu Okumura. 2016. A Corpus-Based Analysis of Canonical Word Order of Japanese Double Object Constructions. In *Proceedings of the 54th Annual Meeting of the Association for Computational Linguistics (Volume 1: Long Papers)*, pages 2236–2244, Berlin, Germany. Association for Computational Linguistics.

Tanner Sorensen, Sven Hohenstein, and Shravan Vasishth. 2016. Bayesian linear mixed models using stan: A tutorial for psychologists, linguists, and cognitive scientists. *Quantitative Methods for Psychology*, 12(3):175–200.

Enric Vallduví and Elisabet Engdahl. 1996. The linguistic realization of information packaging. *Linguistics*, 34(3):459–520.

Reiko Vermeulen. 2012. The information structure of japanese. In Renate Musan Manfred Krifka, editor, *The expression of information structure*, pages 187–216. Berlin: De Gruyter Mouton.

Hiroko Yamashita and Franklin Chang. 2001. "Long Before Short" Preference in the Production of a Head-final Language. *Cognition*, 81(2):B45–B55.

Hiroko Yamashita and Tadahisa Kondo. 2011. Linguistic constraints and long-before-short tendency. In *IEICE Technocal report (TL)*, TL2011-19, pages 61–65.

Affordances in Grounded Language Learning

Stephen McGregor   **KyungTae Lim**

LATTICE - CNRS & École normale supérieure / PSL

Université Sorbonne nouvelle Paris 3 / USPC

1, rue Maurice Arnoux, 92120 Montrouge, France

`semcgregor@hotmail.com`   `kyungtae.lim@ens.fr`

Abstract

We present a novel methodology involving mappings between different modes of semantic representations. We propose distributional semantic models as a mechanism for representing the kind of world knowledge inherent in the system of abstract symbols characteristic of a sophisticated community of language users. Then, motivated by insight from ecological psychology, we describe a model approximating affordances, by which we mean a language learner's direct perception of opportunities for action in an environment. We present a preliminary experiment involving mapping between these two representational modalities, and propose that our methodology can become the basis for a cognitively inspired model of grounded language learning.

1 Introduction

Computational approaches to grounded language learning have typically involved mapping from perceptual to linguistic modalities through the application of complex information processing operations. Yu and Siskind (2013), for instance, use hidden Markov models to translate from *object tracks* to natural language descriptions of event observed in video clips. Likewise the ImageNet database has provided a platform for the productive application of deep neural network architectures for mapping between images and natural language labels (Krizhevsky et al., 2012). Significantly with regard to the ideas outlined here, Oh et al. (2017) describe a methodology for training an agent to construct novel sequences of actions based on analogies with previously learned strategies; the mechanism for learning a vocabulary of basic actions consists of a combination of convolutional and LSTM layers within a neural network.

Work of this nature highlights the state of the art in modelling technologies, and as an information engineering approach to meaningful tasks such as question answering and image labelling a significant contribution is made. This is arguably done, however, at the expense of presenting interpretable or indeed plausible models of the way that environmentally embedded agents use relatively scant exposure to a language speaking community in order to develop a lexicon that is rich and productive. In this regard, the conventional computational stance on grounded language learning embraces a view of the relationship between language and the world as a *symbol grounding problem*, by which abstract symbols susceptible to formal operations are somehow associated with perceptions and propositions: the hard work is done by a complex and philosophically opaque process of transforming signals into symbols, with the sense that computation by way of deep nets in some sense stands in for an inscrutable mind-brain gestalt.

As an alternative to this approach, Rączaszek-Leonardi et al. (2018) propose a *symbol ungrounding problem*: by this account, language begins as a semiotic structure with the representational scheme of a nascent language learner iconically and indexically aligned to embodied and embedded experiences of the world. This alignment is understood in terms of Gibson's (1979) notion of *affordances*, which we take to mean the direct perception of opportunities for action in an environment. The connection of language to opportunities for taking action on objects (and indeed the perception of language itself as an affordance for communication) creates a framework for understanding how abstract symbols begin as grounded complexes of multi-modal interactions with a language teacher and then gradually emerge as con-

41

Proceedings of the Eighth Workshop on Cognitive Aspects of Computational Language Learning and Processing, pages 41–46

Melbourne, Australia, July 19, 2018. ©2018 Association for Computational Linguistics

straints on the way that a cognitive agent behaves in an environment (Rączaszek-Leonardi, 2012).

The strength of thinking of perception in general and language in particular in terms of affordances is that this moves away from the problem of the computational load associated with the spontaneous construction of contextually productive representational structures. For Clark (1997), affordances play a role in the an *action-oriented* model of cognition revolving around light-weight, environmentally situated representations, while Chemero (2009) proposes affordances as a mechanism for resolving the issue of the *mental gymnastics* inherent in a computational cognitive model. These approaches, which seek to place mind in the context of environmental embodiment and embeddedness, prefigure recent attempts to introduce affordances as a component of a cognitively oriented theory of language in which words can be mapped to denotations oriented towards action on objects in situations, and utterances themselves become opportunities for communication (Rączaszek-Leonardi and Nomikou, 2015).

Despite these valuable theoretical contributions, affordances have proved resistant to empirical modelling, not least because it is difficult to come up with a tractable scheme for representing a cognitive feature that is specifically conceived as an antidote to representational approaches to cognition. Our present objective is to begin to map a way towards the computational simulation of the role of affordances in language acquisition through interaction with an established linguistic community. In order to do this, we'll extract both statistical and syntactic information from a large-scale corpus to model two different modes of semantic representation, one geared towards the kind of world-knowledge inherent in the evolution of language on the time-scale of a community of language users, the other designed to reflect the way that an agent might encounter language grounded in the affordances of denoted objects.

In as much as we will be combining established distributional semantic techniques with likewise established syntactic analysis, this work can be broadly positioned in the context of other recent models. Cheng and Kartsaklis (2015), for instance, compound co-occurrence and syntactical information in order to generate word-embeddings enhanced for compositional tasks. Vulić (2017) likewise uses information about dependency re-lationships to map word embeddings from multiple languages into a shared vector space, achieving impressive results on cross-lingual versions of word similarity tasks. An important caveat regarding our own research, however, is that we are using syntactical information as a kind of stand-in for a simulation of the way that an agent might encounter words aligned with events involving objects: in the end, we would actually like to see the methodology outlined here as groundwork towards a model of language acquisition which specifically does not fall back on the kind of rich linguistic knowledge inherent in either vector space models or dependency parsers.

2 Modelling Affordances

On the one hand, as a model for the type of lexical semantic representation imbued with the productive world knowledge of an experienced language user, we propose distributional semantic vector space models (Clark, 2015), in which words are represented as points in high dimensional spaces where properties such as proximity and direction can relate to semantic phenomena such as relatedness and intension. On the other hand, as a model of the perception of objects mapped to linguistic units and at the same time perceived in terms of their potential for being acted upon, we suggest a rudimentary framework for associating denotations with events and related objects.

Distributional semantic word-vectors have the advantage of incorporating both world knowledge (Mikolov et al., 2013; Pennington et al., 2014) and at least the potential for compositionality (Mitchell and Lapata, 2010; Coecke et al., 2011) into a computationally tractable structure. They can also, importantly, be extrapolated in an essentially unsupervised way from large-scale textual data, allowing for the construction of an open ended lexicon characterised by the representation of semantic properties through geometric features. In terms of our framework for modelling a language-learning agent, we propose that this type of representation can stand in for interaction between the agent and a tutor acting as a conduit to the knowledge embedded in a language as developed by a community of language users (Smith et al., 2003).

In terms of actually instantiating this type of model, we apply the `word2vec` technique to learn a space of word embeddings (Mikolov et al.,

2013), applied across iterative observations of a cleaned-up version of Wikipedia.[1] We detect sentence boundaries, remove punctuation, render all characters lower-case, and, ignoring sentences of less than five words in length, apply the *skip-gram* methodology for learning to predict a 5-by-5 window of co-occurrence words around a given target word. The cleaned version of our corpus contains about 9.08 million word types representing roughly 1.87 billion word tokens spread across 87.2 million sentences.

As a model of the way that language is encountered in the environment by a novice language learner, we propose a representational scheme for affordances designed to reflect the actions and interactions that might be associated with an agent's early encounters with new objects. For present purposes, we will once again turn to a corpus-based technique for building representations: we traverse the same rendition of Wikipedia, seeking instances where words in our vocabulary are used as direct objects. We parse each sentence in the corpus using the Spacy parser; in instances of multi-word phrases, we treat the head as a candidate target word. For word types tagged as direct objects, we build up counts of corresponding predicates and associated subjects and indirect objects and then calculate probability distributions over the word types observed in each of these roles, so that affordances can be represented as a matrix of probability distributions over word types for each of these three grammatical classes for every word in a target vocabulary:

$$p(X|w) = \left(\frac{|x_{w,1}|}{|X_w|}, \frac{|x_{w,2}|}{|X_w|} ... \right) \qquad (1)$$

$$w = (p(P|w), p(S|w), p(I|w)) \qquad (2)$$

Here, a distribution $p(X|w)$ represents the discrete probabilities of words $(x_1, x_2...)$ being observed in a dependency relationship X with word w, calculated for predicates, subjects, and indirect objects (P, S, I) respectively. We take these grammatical features to correspond, at least in a rough sense, to the kind of thing that can be done with the corresponding target object, the things that do these things, and the things that can be affected by actions involving this object.

With these probability spaces established, we can compute the top words in terms of probabil-

ity of observation in a particular grammatical role across all vocabulary words up to some arbitrary count. So, for instance, an affordance matrix for the word *taxi* built with three-element probability distributions would look like this (where PRO and YEAR are generic representations for personal pronouns and years respectively):

predicate	subject	ind. object
take = 0.587	PRO = 0.809	YEAR = 0.385
drive = 0.279	*who* = 0.112	*airport* = 0.365
hail = 0.134	*von* = 0.079	*station* = 0.250

3 A Small Experiment

Beginning with the framework described above, we first examine the degree to which our representations capture properties associated with the denotations of some basic nouns. In order to establish a small-scale vocabulary of objects, we turn to the tables of words exemplifying types of objects described by Rosch (1975) in her seminal work on conceptual prototypes. We choose the five words that were reported as most prototypical of five conceptual categories, as determined by a survey of a large number of respondents. The categories are VEHICLES, CLOTHING, TOOLS, FURNITURE, and FRUIT. Our objective for this preliminary work will be to establish representations of these object types in both a distributional semantic vector space and a probabilistic affordance space.

In order to explore the effectiveness of the conceptual spaces generated by the representational techniques described above, we first extract the word-vectors corresponding to our vocabulary from the `word2vec` distributional semantic model and perform k-means clustering on these, specifying a total of five target classes.[2] Results are reported in the WORD-VECTORS column in Table 1. While these clusters do not correspond exactly with human judgement, they do align somewhat with the expected delineations between object classes. The large cluster containing a mix of furniture and tools is characterised by words like *saw* and *ruler* which are presumably affected by a high degree of word sense ambiguity.

Next we explore the space of affordances. The representations in this space are, as described above, construed as matrices of probabilities. Specifically, we take the top 20 most likely words

---

[1] Implemented using the Gensim library for Python.

[2] Clustering is implemented using the KMeans algorithm from Python's sklearn library.

WORD-VECTORS	AFFORDANCES
automobile, truck, car, bus, taxi	**car**, *automobile, truck, taxi*
pants, shirt, dress, skirt, blouse	**dress**, *pants, shirt, skirt, blouse*
hammer, screwdriver	**hammer**, *table, bus, screwdriver, drill*
chair, sofa, couch, table, dresser, saw, ruler, drill	**chair**
orange, apple, banana, peach, pear	**orange**, *sofa, couch, dresser, apple, banana, peach, pear, saw, ruler*

Table 1: Clusters of word representations in distributional semantic and probabilistic affordance spaces. Word-vectors are clustered based on k-means clustering, and affordance representations are clustered based on a k-medoid algorithm, with the most cost-effective medoids indicated in bold.

for each grammatical class and generate probabilities for each word in each of these classes for each of our 25 object-words. In order to calculate the distance between two affordance representations, we take the Hellinger distance between two aligned probability distributions. This operation, which we take as a good quantification of the relationship between two distributions, results in a matrix of three dimensional vectors, each element corresponding to a grammatical class. So, for two vocabulary words a and b and a grammatical class c, the element of a vector representing the relationship between those two words can be described as follows, where h is the label for one of the top 20 words occurring in that grammatical class:

$$M_c(a,b) = \frac{1}{\sqrt{2}} \times \sqrt{\sum_{h=1}^{20} \left(\sqrt{p(a_h)} - \sqrt{p(b_h)} \right)^2} \tag{3}$$

We treat the set of three values corresponding to each target-to-target relationship as a distance vector, and so consider the distance between those two words to be simply the norm of that vector. With a distance matrix thus established, we use a k-medoids algorithm of our own design to cluster the affordance representations. We apply this measure because we are working from a matrix of distances, rather than from an explicit vector space; we might also consider, for instance, multi-dimensional scaling to project these representations into a vector space, but we consider the k-medoid approach to be appropriate for our present purposes. Results are reported in the right column of Table 1, with optimal medoids highlighted.

As with the clustering of word-vectors, the results here do not correspond perfectly with human judgements. We don't see this as necessarily being a problem, though: it would be strange, in fact, to expect a developing cognitive agent to categor-

ically classify each object based on affordance-oriented interactions with an environment. So, for instance, fruits are compounded with some furniture and some tools in a single category orbiting the highly ambiguous term *orange*.

The crucial question is how we can effectively map between word-vectors, which we take to represent a kind of encyclopaedic knowledge of the world, and the affordances which are proposed as at least a rough model of the way that words are encountered by an early language learner. In order to explore this issue further, we construct a rudimentary neural network, mapping the 200 elements of each of our word-vectors onto the sets of probability distributions corresponding to affordances by way of a single dense softmax layer. This operation is in effect quite similar to a multi-class logistic regression, except that here we are attempting to learn to approximate an actual probability distribution rather than to simply reward the assignment of the highest score to a particular class. Formally, we map from a word-vector $\overrightarrow{v_w}$ to a probability distribution $p(x_n|w)$ associated with a word x_n observed participating with vocabulary word w as a member of grammatical class X by learning a weight matrix M, expressed here in terms of dot products with each row $\overrightarrow{m_{x_k}}$ associated with members $(x_1...x_{|X|})$ of class X:

$$p(x_n|w) = \frac{e^{\overrightarrow{v_w}^T \cdot \overrightarrow{m_{x_n}}}}{\sum_{k=1}^{k=|X|} e^{\overrightarrow{v_w}^T \cdot \overrightarrow{m_{x_k}}}} \tag{4}$$

A separate weight matrix is learned for each of the three grammatical classes associate with the objects that we seek to model.

As a basic test of the generality of this network, we perform a five-fold cross-validation, holding one term from each class out of the network construction process for each fold. Table 2 reports accuracy rates for this experiment, where a word-

	TOTAL	VEHICLES	CLOTHING	TOOLS	FURNITURE	FRUIT
word	0.12	0.0	0.2	0.2	0.2	0.0
class	0.64	0.8	0.6	0.6	0.2	1.0

Table 2: Accuracy rates for mapping from distributional semantic word-vectors to affordance matrices, from a word to the same word and from a word to another word of the same class.

vector is considered to map to the point in the space of affordance matrices that is closest based on Hellinger as technique described above. This experiment is designed to test the ability of this simple model to map between two different modes of semantic representation, one based on a large-scale analysis of the way that words occur in the context of a complex, developed vocabulary, the other utilising syntax to simulate the small-scale encounter of words as mapping to opportunities for action on corresponding denotations.

While the network generally fails to make exact word-to-word mappings, it is notable that it does, more often than not, manage to map a word-vector to an affordance representation corresponding to another word of at least the correct class. We suggest that this indicates there is some basic categorical information in word-vector representations that can be aligned with data about the way that objects are predictably encountered in the world.

4 What Next?

The development of a mapping between encyclopaedic and empirical lexical semantic representations described here is, in the end, not particular remarkable. We have in effect mapped from one statistical interpretation of a corpus to another. There is a large space of parameters to toggle: the parameters of the `word2vec` methodology for generating word-vectors, the number and choice of grammatical classes for our affordance space, the actual selection of target vocabulary words, and the network architecture for mapping between representational frameworks are just some of the factors inviting further experimentation.

Moreover, the experiments we carry out involve a small set of words distributed over a likewise small set of classes. This is in contrast to some of the more ambitious approaches to multi-modal tasks such as image labelling that have recently emerged, which can involve thousands of labels (Frome et al., 2013). What we are aiming at, though, is not so much an approach to information engineering as a first step towards modelling the way grounded language learning might happen for an environmentally situated agent.

To this end, there is ample room to reconsider the way in which we model affordances in the first place. The corpus-based technique described here is amenable to a computational approach, but ultimately it will be important to develop a more situated methodology. To this end, experiments on human-robot interaction conducted by (Gross and Krenn, 2016) have illustrated the way in which factors such as gaze and gesture are crucial features of early-stage linguistic interactions, and we suggest that a mechanism for representing these elements of communication is an important consideration in modelling grounded language learning. Likewise with a focus on robotic applications, Spranger and Steels (2014) have explored the way that the *ontogentic ritualisation* inherent in the phenotype of a community of language users plays an important role in human language learning.

Returning to more traditionally computational tasks, we finally propose that an affordance based model can play a useful role in mapping between low-level input from, for instance, the visual domain and more abstract linguistic representations. What we have described here might be conceived as one wing of the type of autoencoder network that has been successful in tasks involving image processing (Krizhevsky et al., 2012) and machine translation (Hill et al., 2016). Rather than treating the encoding at the locus of these networks as an arbitrarily abstract semantic representation, we propose that an effective system might involve encoding to and decoding from affordance type representations. The next step in exploring this hypothesis will be to experiment with mapping from images to affordances. We have no illusions that this will be an easy task, but we do think that we have established sufficient groundwork for carrying ahead with this line of research.

Acknowledgements

This work was supported by the ERA-NET Atlantis project.

References

Anthony Chemero. 2009. *Radical Embodied Cognitive Science*. The MIT Press, Cambridge, MA.

Jianpeng Cheng and Dimitri Kartsaklis. 2015. Syntax-aware multi-sense word embeddings for deep compositional models of meaning. In *Proceedings of the 2015 Conference on Empirical Methods in Natural Language Processing*, pages 1531–1542. Association for Computational Linguistics.

Andy Clark. 1997. *Being There: Putting Brain, Body, and World Together Again*. MIT Press, Cambridge, MA.

Stephen Clark. 2015. Vector space models of lexical meaning. In Shalom Lappin and Chris Fox, editors, *The Handbook of Contemporary Semantic Theory*, pages 493–522. Wiley-Blackwell.

Bob Coecke, Mehrnoosh Sadrzadeh, and Stephen Clark. 2011. Mathematical foundations for a compositional distributed model of meaning. *Linguistic Analysis*, 36(1-4):345–384.

Andrea Frome, Greg S Corrado, Jon Shlens, Samy Bengio, Jeff Dean, Marc Aurelio Ranzato, and Tomas Mikolov. 2013. DeViSE: A deep visual-semantic embedding model. In C. J. C. Burges, L. Bottou, M. Welling, Z. Ghahramani, and K. Q. Weinberger, editors, *Advances in Neural Information Processing Systems 26*, pages 2121–2129.

James J. Gibson. 1979. *The Ecological Approach to Visual Perception*. Houghton Miffline, Boston.

Stephanie Gross and Brigitte Krenn. 2016. The ofai multi-modal task description corpus. In *Proceedings of the Tenth International Conference on Language Resources and Evaluation (LREC)*.

Felix Hill, Kyunghyun Cho, and Anna Korhonen. 2016. Learning distributed representations of sentences from unlabelled data. In *Proceedings of the 2016 Conference of the North American Chapter of the Association for Computational Linguistics: Human Language Technologies*, pages 1367–1377. Association for Computational Linguistics.

Alex Krizhevsky, Ilya Sutskever, and Geoffrey E. Hinton. 2012. Imagenet classification with deep convolutional neural networks. In *Proceedings of the 25th International Conference on Neural Information Processing Systems - Volume 1*, pages 1097–1105.

Tomas Mikolov, Kai Chen, Greg Corrado, and Jeffrey Dean. 2013. Efficient estimation of word representations in vector space. In *Proceedings of ICLR Workshop*.

Jeff Mitchell and Mirella Lapata. 2010. Composition in distributional models of semantics. *Cognitive Science*, 34(8):1388–1439.

Junhyuk Oh, Satinder P. Singh, Honglak Lee, and Pushmeet Kohli. 2017. Zero-shot task generalization with multi-task deep reinforcement learning. In *Proceedings of the 34th International Conference on Machine Learning*, pages 2661–2670.

Jeffrey Pennington, Richard Socher, and Christopher D. Manning. 2014. GloVe: Global vectors for word representation. In *Conference on Empirical Methods in Natural Language Processing*.

Joanna Rączaszek-Leonardi. 2012. Language as a system of replicable constraints. In Howar Hunt Pattee and Joanna Rączaszek-Leonardi, editors, *Laws, Lanuage and Life*, pages 295–333. Springer.

Joanna Rączaszek-Leonardi and Iris Nomikou. 2015. Beyond mechanistic interaction: Value-based constraints on meaning in language. *Frontiers in Psychology*, 6(1579).

Joanna Rączaszek-Leonardi, Iris Nomikou, Katharina J. Rohlfing, and Terrence W. Deacon. 2018. Language development from an ecological perspective: Ecologically valid ways to abstract symbols. *Ecological Psychology*, 30(1):39–73.

Eleanor Rosch. 1975. Cognitive representations of semantic categories. *Journal of Experimental Psychology: General*, 104:192–233.

Kenny Smith, Henry Brighton, and Simon Kirby. 2003. Complex systems in language evolution: The cultural emergence of compositional structure. *Advances in Complex Systems*, 6(4):537–558.

Michael Spranger and Luc Steels. 2014. Discovering communication through ontogenetic ritualisation. In *4th International Conference on Development and Learning and on Epigenetic Robotics (ICDL-EPIROB)*, pages 14–19.

Ivan Vulić. 2017. Cross-lingual syntactically informed distributed word representations. In *Proceedings of the 15th Conference of the European Chapter of the Association for Computational Linguistics, EACL 2017, Valencia, Spain, April 3-7, 2017, Volume 2: Short Papers*, pages 408–414.

Haonan Yu and Jeffrey Mark Siskind. 2013. Grounded language learning from video described with sentences. In *Proceedings of the 51st Annual Meeting of the Association for Computational Linguistics*, pages 53–63.

Rating Distributions and Bayesian Inference:
Enhancing Cognitive Models of Spatial Language Use

Thomas Kluth
Language & Cognition Group
CITEC, Bielefeld University
Inspiration 1, 33619 Bielefeld
Germany
tkluth@cit-ec.uni-bielefeld.de

Holger Schultheis
Bremen Spatial Cognition Center
University of Bremen
Enrique-Schmidt-Str. 5, 28359 Bremen
Germany
schulth@uni-bremen.de

Abstract

We present two methods that improve the assessment of cognitive models. The first method is applicable to models computing average acceptability ratings. For these models, we propose an extension that simulates a full rating distribution (instead of average ratings) and allows generating individual ratings. Our second method enables Bayesian inference for models generating individual data. To this end, we propose to use the cross-match test (Rosenbaum, 2005) as a likelihood function. We exemplarily present both methods using cognitive models from the domain of spatial language use. For spatial language use, determining linguistic acceptability judgments of a spatial preposition for a depicted spatial relation is assumed to be a crucial process (Logan and Sadler, 1996). Existing models of this process compute an average acceptability rating. We extend the models and – based on existing data – show that the extended models allow extracting more information from the empirical data and yield more readily interpretable information about model successes and failures. Applying Bayesian inference, we find that model performance relies less on mechanisms of capturing geometrical aspects than on mapping the captured geometry to a rating interval.

1 Introduction

Acceptability judgments are an important measure throughout linguistic research (Sprouse, 2013). For instance, Alhama et al. (2015) recently proposed to use confidence ratings to assess models of artificial language learning. Likewise, in research on the evaluation of spatial language given visual displays, a common experimental paradigm is to ask how well a spatial term describes a depicted situation (e.g., Regier and Carlson, 2001; Logan and Sadler, 1996; Burigo et al., 2016; Hörberg, 2008). This paradigm results in individual acceptability judgments on Likert scales. These rating data are the main source for assessing computational models in the spatial language domain (e.g., Regier and Carlson, 2001; Coventry et al., 2005; Kluth and Schultheis, 2014). In other linguistic domains, similar empirical rating data are predicted by computational models (e.g., grammaticality judgments, Lau et al., 2017, or semantic plausibility judgments Padó et al., 2009; see also Chater and Manning, 2006).

Generally speaking, researchers consider a rating-model appropriate if it can closely account for empirical mean ratings for the given stimuli (averaged across subjects) – the closer the fit to the empirical mean data, the more appropriate the model. However, the use of mean ratings instead of full rating distributions misses the opportunity to use all available empirical information for model assessment. This is why we present a model extension that adds the simulation of a probability distribution over all ratings. We illustrate our extension by equipping spatial language models with full empirical rating distributions.

The second proposal of our paper (Bayesian inference) relies on the fact that our proposed model extension enables the generation of individual ratings by sampling from the simulated probability distribution. This opens up the possibility to apply Bayesian inference (e.g., to reason about the likely values of model parameters). Many cognitive models lack a likelihood function that specifies how likely the empirical data are given a specific parameter set. This prevents the use of Bayesian inference. In this contribution, we propose the

Proceedings of the Eighth Workshop on Cognitive Aspects of Computational Language Learning and Processing, pages 47–55
Melbourne, Australia, July 19, 2018. ©2018 Association for Computational Linguistics

cross-match test developed by (Rosenbaum, 2005) as a means for computing the likelihood for cognitive models that are able to generate individual data.

Again, we use a spatial language model to exemplify the application of the cross-match method. The thus computed posterior distribution of the model's parameters has surprising implications for the interpretation of the model. Before we come to this, we start with presenting the example models, followed by our model extension to simulate rating distributions.

1.1 Exemplary Spatial Language Models

We introduce both our methods by exemplarily applying them to the AVS model (Regier and Carlson, 2001) and the recently proposed AVS-BB, rAVS, and rAVS-CoO models (Kluth et al., 2017, under revision). Given a depicted spatial layout and a spatial sentence ("The [located object] is above the [reference object]"), these cognitive models generate mean acceptability ratings, i.e., judgments how well the linguistic input describes the visual scene. All models can be interpreted as consisting of two components: One component that captures geometric aspects of the depicted spatial configuration and one component that maps the captured geometry to a rating interval (representing linguistic acceptability judgments).

The models process geometry by defining vectors on all points of one object of the spatial layout. These vectors point to the second object in the layout. In addition, each vector is weighted by a certain amount of attention defined by a spotlight-like distribution of attention. The overall direction of the vector *sum* is compared to a reference direction (e.g., canonical upright for the preposition *above*). This angular deviation is the outcome of the first model component (processing geometry).

The first model component is where the two model families (AVS & AVS-BB vs. rAVS & rAVS-CoO) differ: The AVS and the AVS-BB models assume a shift of attention from the reference object to the located object (the vectors point from the reference object to the located object). In contrast, the rAVS and rAVS-CoO models assume a reversed shift of attention from the located object to the reference object (hence their acronym: *reversed* AVS; the vectors point from the located object to the reference object). The difference within the model families (i.e., AVS vs. AVS-BB and rAVS

vs. rAVS-CoO) will be introduced in Section 3.

The second model component is the same in all models: A linear function that maps the angular deviation from the first component to a rating interval. In Section 4.2.1 we introduce some details about the role of rAVS-CoO's parameters for the two model components. Applying our model extension and the second proposal of our paper (Bayesian inference), we present evidence that the second component of the models (mapping geometry to rating) seems to be more important than the first one (processing geometry).

2 Model Extension: Rating Distributions

As an illustrating example of our model extension, consider the empirical rating distribution displayed as bars in Fig. 1c. This distribution shows 34 acceptability ratings on a rating scale with $K = 9$ categories (from 1–9). These ratings come from an empirical study by Kluth et al. (under revision) in which they asked 34 participants to judge the acceptability of the German sentence "Der Punkt ist über dem Objekt" ("The dot is above the object"). Specifically, the distribution shown in Fig. 1c corresponds to empirical ratings for the left black dot above the asymmetrical object depicted in Fig. 1a.

Our method of simulating such a rating distribution is inspired by a common approach of analyzing ordinal data (i.e., discrete and ordered data) using generalized linear (regression) models (e.g., Liddell and Kruschke, 2018; Kruschke, 2015, chapter 23). Here, the cumulative probability of a latent Gaussian distribution between two thresholds is the probability of one specific rating k (see Fig. 1c).[1] Based on this, we propose the following steps to extend mean-rating-models with the ability of simulating full rating distributions:

1. Interpret the output of the model as the mean μ of a Gaussian distribution (see maximum of dashed curve in Fig. 1c or 1d).

2. Treat σ of the Gaussian distribution and $K - 1 - 2$ thresholds as additional model parameters (see width of dashed curve and vertical lines in Fig. 1c or 1d; K is the number of all outcomes; first and last thresholds have fixed values).

3. Define a discrete probability distribution over all K ratings like in an ordinal regression (i.e,

---

[1] For the first / last outcome it is the cumulative probability between negative / positive infinity and the first / last threshold.

cumulative probabilities of the Gaussian distribution between thresholds, see model outputs in Fig. 1c or 1d).

4. To generate an individual rating: Sample a rating from the discrete probability distribution defined in the previous step.

Note that the discrete probability distribution over all K ratings defined in step 3 is fully determined by the model parameters (i.e., it will not change unless you change any of the model parameters) while the individual rating generated in step 4 is subject to sampling noise.

To fit such an extended model to empirical data, we compute the Kullback-Leibler divergence from the model's discrete probability distribution (see model outputs in Fig. 1c or 1d) to the empirical rating distribution (relative frequencies of ratings, see bars in Fig. 1c or 1d) – for every dot-object pair that served as a stimulus. Then we minimize the mean Kullback-Leibler divergence (averaged over all stimuli). This procedure requires that individual empirical data are available.

Note that this approach of comparing model outputs to empirical data still operates on the data from all study participants (but it uses more information as it does not operate only on a mean value). That is, instead of explicitly assessing the models on individual behavior, our fitting approach aims to capture the overall rating distribution. Given that with our model extension a model may also generate individual outcomes, it is in principle possible to explicitly model single individuals or groups of individuals with similar rating patterns. We leave this for future work and note that the work from Navarro et al. (2006) might prove valuable for this endeavor.

3 Results: Fitting Models to Rating Distributions

To exemplarily apply our proposed model extension, we extended the AVS model (Regier and Carlson, 2001) as well as the recently proposed AVS-BB, rAVS, and rAVS-CoO models (Kluth et al., 2017, under revision) and fitted them to empirical data from Kluth et al. (under revision, asymmetrical objects only). We denote the extended models with a trailing + (see labels in Fig. 1). The source code and all data are available under open licenses (GNU GPL and ODbL) from Kluth (2018).

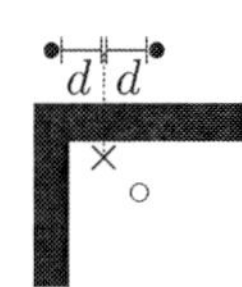

(a) Spatial configuration with two exemplary dot locations used in acceptability rating study by Kluth et al. (under revision). $\times$ = center-of-mass, $\circ$ = center-of-object (of the asymmetrical object); d = same horizontal distance from $\times$ for both dots. Participants saw only one dot and the asymmetrical object (neither the centers nor the additional lines shown here).

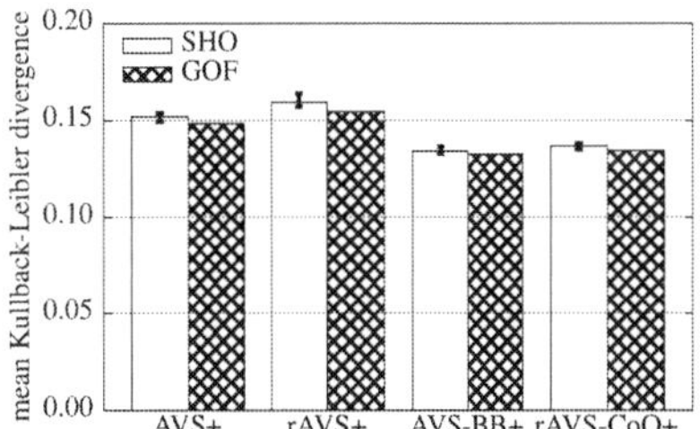

(b) Goodness-of-fit (GOF) and simple hold-out (SHO) results for fitting extended models to whole empirical rating distribution from Kluth et al. (under revision, 4 asymmetrical objects $\times$ 28 dots $\times$ 2 prepositions = 224 data points). Error bars show 95% confidence intervals of SHO medians.

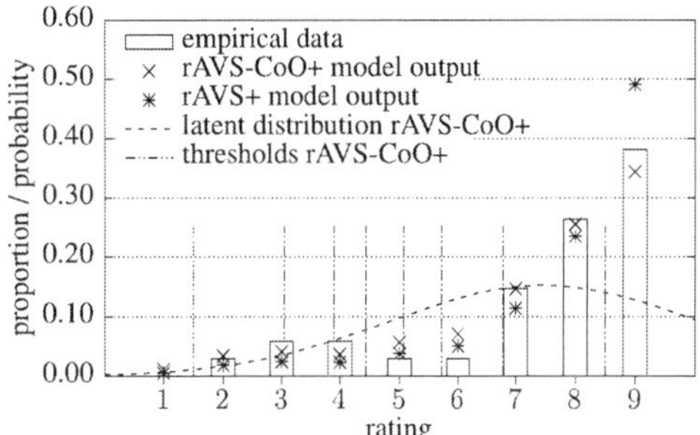

(c) Empirical "über" ("above") rating distribution and model probabilities (rAVS+ and rAVS-CoO+) for the **left dot** shown in Fig. 1a. Model probabilities were computed using the parameters from the best fit plotted in Fig. 1b. Participants never chose rating 1.

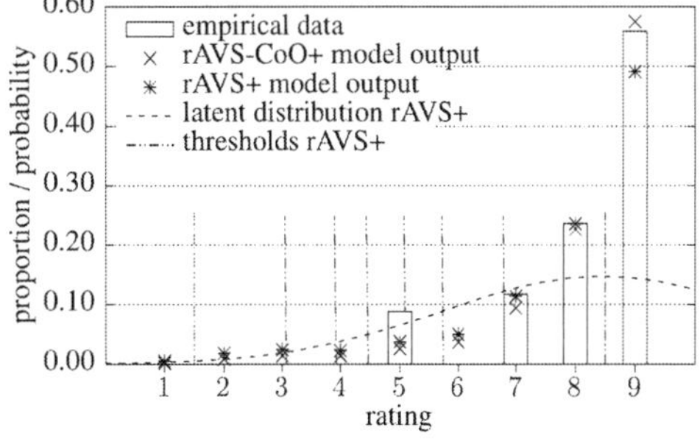

(d) Empirical "über" ("above") rating distribution and model probabilities (rAVS+ and rAVS-CoO+) for the **right dot** shown in Fig. 1a. Model probabilities were computed using the parameters from the best fit plotted in Fig. 1b. Participants never chose ratings 1-4 or 6.

Figure 1: Example experimental display, fits of extended models, and empirical rating distributions.

Given a depicted spatial configuration containing a geometric object and a single dot placed above / below the object (see Fig. 1a), we asked 34 German native speakers to rate the acceptability of the German sentences "Der Punkt ist über dem Objekt" and "Der Punkt ist unter dem Objekt" ("The dot is above / below the object") on a Likert scale from 1–9 (with lower ratings coding lower acceptability judgments). We placed 28 dots above and 28 dots below 4 asymmetrical objects (i.e., the whole data set consists of 224 data points; for the current work we did not consider data from additionally tested rectangular reference objects).

Fig. 1a shows two exemplary dot locations above one of the used asymmetrical objects. For these two dots, we expected participants to give equal "über" ("above") acceptability ratings (based on earlier research, e.g., Regier and Carlson, 2001). However, we found that participants rated the acceptability of the "über" ("above") sentence for the right dot in Fig. 1a higher than for the left dot (Kluth et al., under revision). This finding generalized reliably to different objects with similar dot placements suggesting that people possibly prefer the center-of-object (depicted as ○ in Fig. 1a) over the center-of-mass (depicted as × in Fig. 1a) for their judgments. To account for this finding, Kluth et al. (under revision) proposed the model refinements AVS-BB and rAVS-CoO (AVS-bounding-box and rAVS-center-of-object), which both use the center-of-object instead of the center-of-mass (as AVS and rAVS do) for their computations.

Here, we use the two dot locations depicted in Fig. 1a to exemplarily present our approach of simulating rating distributions. To do so, we first extended all models with the ability to simulate rating distributions and then fitted all extended models to the 224 data points (by minimizing the mean Kullback-Leibler divergence as described above). These fits are plotted in Fig. 1b (as goodness-of-fit values alongside with the outcome of 101 simple hold-out iterations, a cross-validation measure to control for overfitting, Schultheis et al., 2013). In terms of relative model performances, these fits confirm the results of simpler fits using only averaged rating data reported in Kluth et al. (under revision): Both models that take the center-of-object into account (the AVS-BB+ and the rAVS-CoO+ models) fit the data more closely (lower mean Kullback-Leibler divergence) than the models that consider the center-of-mass (AVS+ and rAVS+).

More interesting for our current purpose are the plots in Figs. 1c and 1d. These plots each depict the empirical rating distributions for one of the two dots in Fig. 1a as bars: Fig. 1c shows the distribution for the left dot while Fig. 1d depicts the distribution for the right dot. The empirical distributions show that the left dot received considerably less "9" ratings and more "2–7" ratings compared to the right dot. On top of the empirical distributions, we plotted the probabilities of each rating as computed with the rAVS+ and the rAVS-CoO+ models. To compute these probabilities, we used the parameters found by fitting the models to the whole data set (cf. Fig. 1b). Despite being fit to a much larger data set, the two plots show that both models generally capture the qualitative trend of each of the two single empirical data points. Considering Fig. 1c and Fig. 1d suggests that the rAVS-CoO+ model better accounts for the data – confirming (and explaining, see Kluth et al., under revision) the better fit on the larger data set shown in Fig. 1b.

Fitting the models to rating distributions allows for a more fine-grained model assessment compared to model fits to averaged data. For example, the main source of the different performances of the rAVS+ and the rAVS-CoO+ models seems to be their ability to account for the frequency of the highest rating "9" (cf. Fig. 1c and Fig. 1d). Compare this with the situation where only averaged data is used: Here the only information are mean ratings (for the left dot 7.38, for the right dot 8.18) and fits of the models to these mean ratings. Using the same parameter settings as before, this yields for the left dot 0.1326 (rAVS fit, normalized root mean square error: nRMSE[2]) or 0.0093 (rAVS-CoO fit, nRMSE) and for the right dot 0.0333 (rAVS fit, nRMSE) or 0.1029 (rAVS-CoO fit, nRMSE). None of these numbers provides information about the models' properties as intuitive and informative as the fit of the extended models using full rating distributions. Moreover, our extension also enables the generation of individual data by sampling from the models' discrete rating distribution (see step 4 on page 3). This property can be used to analyze the models with Bayesian inference as we show next.

---

[2] $RMSE = \sqrt{\frac{1}{n}\sum_i^n (data_i - modelOutput_i)^2}$
$nRMSE = RMSE/(rating_{max} - rating_{min})$

4 Method: Bayesian Inference

The Bayesian framework is a fruitful and theoretically sound approach to reason with probability distributions over model parameters. However, this framework requires that the analyzed model can be interpreted in a probabilistic sense. As for many other cognitive models, this is not the case for any of the models discussed here (AVS, AVS-BB, rAVS, rAVS-CoO or their extended versions) because they lack a likelihood function that specifies how likely empirical data are given a model with a specific parameter set. We propose to use the cross-match test developed by Rosenbaum (2005) as the likelihood function of cognitive models that are able to generate individual data (e.g., the derivatives of the AVS+ model).

4.1 Cross-match Test

The cross-match test is a statistical test that computes the probability of whether multivariate responses of two differently treated subject groups come from the same distribution. In our case, the first group are empirical individual data and the second group are model-generated individual data (see top and bottom of Tab. 1), so the cross-match test becomes a measure of how likely it is that the model-generated data come from the same distribution as the empirical data. Given that we can only change the model-generated data (by using different parameter sets), this amounts to a likelihood function.

Internally, the cross-match test is based on grouping the multivariate responses (rows in Tab. 1) into pairs with minimal distances (Mahalanobis distances of ranks). The more of these pairs "cross-match" between the two groups, the more similar are the data of the two groups and hence the higher is the probability that the cross-match test computes (for more details see Rosenbaum, 2005).

4.2 Estimating the Posterior Distribution

To apply the cross-match test as a likelihood function of AVS+ derivatives, we propose the following procedure[3]:

1. For each stimulus, simulate as many ratings with the model as there were participants in

data type	left dot	right dot	...
empirical	7	8	...
empirical	9	9	...
...	...	...	...
model	8	9	...
model	5	8	...
...	...	...	...

Table 1: Example input for the cross-match test (Rosenbaum, 2005). Each row describes the response of one subject (empirical or model-generated), each column describes the response to a stimulus (e.g., the left or right dot from Fig. 1a).

   the study by applying the procedure of generating individual ratings described in step 4 on page 3.

2. Compute the cross-match test comparing the empirical data with the model-generated data.

3. To account for sampling noise (see step 4 on page 3 in the generation of individual data) and provide reliable cross-match results for the same model parameters:

   (a) For every individual rating to be generated in step 1, sample s times and use the mean outcome as generated rating.

   (b) Use the following average of cross-match computations as likelihood value:

      i. Compute the mean number of cross-matches from c cross-match tests and store the probability for this number of cross-matches.

      ii. Repeat step i for b blocks and use the mean of these b probabilities as the likelihood value.

Step 3 (b) basically repeats steps 1 and 2 $b \cdot c$ times. In our case, we found a sufficiently stable likelihood by applying step 3 with $s = 10$, $b = 20$, and $c = 4$ (standard error of averaged cross-match result < 0.05). Note that a too large value of s will generate model outputs that are too similar to each other and thus possibly reduces the number of cross-matches too much. The problem of an unstable likelihood value will reduce when more empirical individual data are available.

Having the likelihood function defined in this way, one can apply standard Markov Chain Monte

---

[3]Note that for clarity of presentation we stay in our exemplary domain: rating-models for spatial language. In principle, our approach is applicable to all models that are able to generate individual data points (not necessarily ratings).

Carlo (MCMC) techniques to estimate the posterior distribution. Specifically, we implemented a Metropolis-Hastings algorithm and improved its performance by adding the adaptation algorithm proposed by Garthwaite et al. (2016). For the cross-match test, we used the R package `crossmatch` (Heller et al., 2012) and re-implemented parts of it using the C++ library `Armadillo` (Sanderson and Curtin, 2016). The R package `ggmcmc` (Fernández-i Marín, 2016) helped in visualizing and analyzing the MCMC samples. Again, all source code is available under the GNU GPL license from (Kluth, 2018).

4.2.1 Example rAVS-CoO+: Model Parameters & Prior Distributions

We exemplarily estimated the posterior distribution of the parameters of the rAVS-CoO+ model. The rAVS-CoO+ model has four free parameters (not considering the additional parameters of our ordinal model extension: σ and thresholds). The two parameters α and $highgain$ are part of the component that processes the geometry of the depicted spatial configuration (cf. Section 1.1). In particular α controls the extraction of an angular deviation from the spatial relation. This angular deviation is mapped to a linguistic rating with the second component of the model. Specifically, high angular deviation results in a low rating and low angular deviation results in a high rating. This is realized with a linear function that maps angular deviation to rating. The $intercept$ and $slope$ parameters are the parameters of this linear function.

Since this is the first study that investigates probability distributions over the model parameters of the rAVS-CoO+ model, we had no prior information available about the likely values of the model parameters. Accordingly, we used uniform distributions within the following parameter ranges as "uninformative" prior distributions:

$$\alpha \in [0.001, 5]; \quad highgain \in [0, 10]$$
$$intercept \in [0.7, 1.3]; \quad slope \in [-1/45, 0]$$

5 Results: Bayesian Inference

We exemplarily estimated the posterior distribution of the parameters of the rAVS-CoO+ model for the same data set to which we fitted the model earlier (consisting of ratings for dots above / below asymmetrical objects, see Fig. 1b for model fits). We used 4 MCMC chains with 125,000 samples in each chain and checked the chains for convergence by monitoring the potential scale reduction factor $\hat{R}$ (Gelman and Rubin, 1992). To obtain converging chains, we had to change the parameterization of the $slope$ parameter to measure "change per radian" instead of "change per degree". Furthermore, we kept the additional model parameters for the ordinal regression (σ of the latent Gaussian distribution and thresholds) constant on the values of the best rAVS-CoO+ fit to the whole data set, because we were primarily interested in the original model parameters. This parameter reduction improved the convergence of the MCMC chains while it did not affect the qualitative results. The results of the posterior estimation are plotted as density estimates of the marginal posterior distribution for each model parameter of the rAVS-CoO+ model in Fig. 2. The different colors code the different MCMC chains. The high overlap of the colors confirms the convergence of the chains.

At a first glance, the marginal posterior distributions are surprising as they lack clear maxima for any parameter in the considered ranges. In particular the α and the $highgain$ parameter seem to have little effect on the model output in terms of generating data similar to empirical data. On the other hand, the marginal posterior distributions suggest that the following regions in the parameter space should result in relatively poor model performance: $\alpha < 0.5$, $intercept > 1.0$, and $slope > -0.25$.

To double-check these regions, we picked two parameter sets and computed the model fits to the empirical data with these parameters (mean Kullback-Leibler divergence). The first parameter set lies in the presumably bad-performance region ($highgain = 5.0, \alpha = 0.2, intercept = 1.25, slope = -0.05$) while the second parameter set consists of parameter values from regions with high posterior density ($highgain = 5.0, \alpha = 3.0, intercept = 0.9, slope = -0.625$). Indeed, the presumably bad-performing parameter set fits the data worse than the other parameter set (mean Kullback-Leibler divergence: 0.484 vs. 0.266, respectively). This trend was confirmed with fits of the same parameter sets using mean ratings instead of rating distributions (nRMSE for worse parameters 0.301 vs. 0.145 for better parameters). These tests provide evidence that using the cross-match test as a likelihood function appropriately captures model performance.

After establishing the validity of the unexpected results, we discuss what we can learn from them.

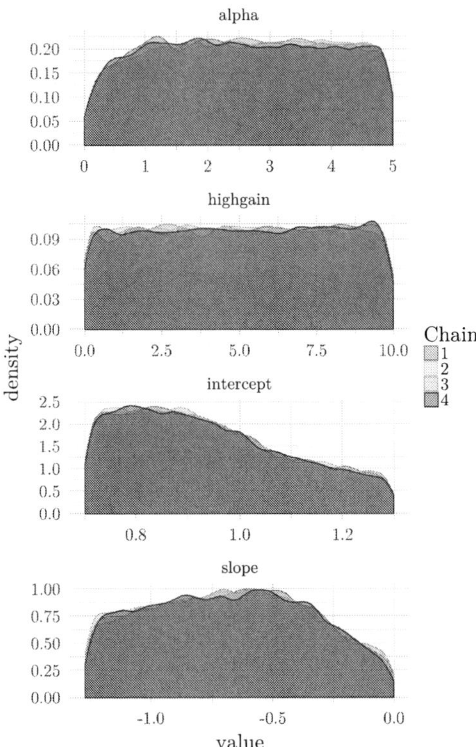

Figure 2: Marginal posterior distributions for the rAVS-CoO+ model given rating data from Kluth et al. (under revision, asymmetrical objects only) and "uninformative" prior distributions (uniform distributions).

Keep in mind that the following conclusions are only valid for the exemplary data set and model for which we computed the posterior estimation and may change with data highlighting different aspects of spatial language use.

Despite the great range of the parameter *highgain* its value does not affect the model performance. Accordingly, the parameter *highgain* seems to be irrelevant for the quality of the model output. Almost the same is true for the parameter α, although the marginal posterior distribution shows weak performance for values less than 0.5. The role of the parameter α in the rAVS-CoO+ model can be understood as an importance weight of two geometric features known to affect spatial language acceptability judgments: the proximal orientation and the center-of-object orientation (Regier and Carlson, 2001; Kluth et al., under revision). The closer α is to 0.0, the more important gets the proximal orientation and the less important gets the center-of-object orientation for the rAVS-CoO+ model. Thus, the marginal posterior distribution provides evidence that the center-of-object orientation is more important than the proximal orientation to account for this data set.

The *intercept* and *slope* parameters control the second model component (cf. Section 1.1): they are the parameters of a linear function contained in the rAVS-CoO+ model that maps angular deviation to rating (between 0 and 1). These two parameters have a greater influence on model performance than α and *highgain* (more diverse posterior profiles for *intercept* and *slope* compared to α and *highgain*, see Figure 2). That is, changing the values of the *intercept* or *slope* parameters affects the models' ability to fit empirical data more strongly than changing the values of α or *highgain*.

This is interesting, because one can interpret the rAVS-CoO+ model (and related models such as AVS+, AVS-BB+, rAVS+) as consisting of (i) a geometric component (capturing / formalizing the geometric properties of the involved objects and their spatial relation) and (ii) a mapping component (mapping the captured geometric aspects onto a rating range, see Section 1.1). Given that one of the prime research question motivating the development of these models concerns the influence of geometric properties (such as relative spatial location of the objects or asymmetrical objects) on spatial language use, most researchers focused on the geometric component of the models. Our results, however, suggest that the geometric component may be less important for model performance than commonly assumed – in particular, less important than the mapping component. That is, to unravel effects of geometry on spatial language use, it might be more insightful to re-consider the mapping of assumed intermediate geometric representations (e.g., angular deviations) to linguistic judgments instead of modeling the computation of these representations.

6 Discussion & Conclusion

Acceptability judgments are common in linguistic research (Sprouse, 2013). Many cognitive models of linguistic processes compute mean acceptability ratings. We propose a model extension that enables these models (i) to simulate a probability distribution over all possible ratings and (ii) to generate individual ratings. To fit simulated probability distributions to empirical rating distributions, we propose to minimize the mean Kullback-Leibler divergence from the simulated to the empirical distributions. This model extension moves the model fits on a level that is closer to the actual empirical data (by using full rating distributions instead of mean ratings) while it avoids the problematic treatment of ordinal data as metric (Liddell and Kruschke, 2018). As future steps in this direction, we envision an analysis whether the additional model parameters can be mapped onto cognitive structures and mechanisms and subsequently the explicit modeling of (groups of) individuals (e.g, via Navarro et al., 2006).

Since many cognitive models lack a likelihood function, our additional contribution is to introduce the cross-match test (Rosenbaum, 2005) as a possible approximation of the likelihood function. This adds the possibility to apply full Bayesian inference for the parameters of all cognitive models that are able to generate individual data (e.g., mean-rating-models enhanced with our model extension).

In the related work of Approximate Bayesian Computation (ABC, for review see Turner and Van Zandt, 2012), researchers have developed sampling strategies to enable "likelihood-free inference". These techniques enable a modeler to use the Bayesian toolkit without explicitly defining a likelihood function. However, ABC sampling algorithms add additional overhead to the workflow of cognitive modelers, as they diverge from standard MCMC techniques used in Bayesian estimations. To overcome this overhead, we propose to use the cross-match test as an explicit likelihood function. We are currently evaluating our approach in comparison to existing ABC algorithms.

We exemplarily applied both our proposals using computational cognitive models of spatial language use like the AVS model (Regier and Carlson, 2001) and its derivatives (Kluth et al., 2017, under revision). Given a depicted spatial layout and a spatial preposition, these models compute mean acceptability ratings. We showed that simulating rating distributions allows a more fine-grained model assessment compared to model fits using mean ratings.

An example application of Bayesian inference revealed surprising insights: We estimated the posterior distribution of rAVS-CoO+'s parameters and found that the values of almost all parameters were less important for model performance than we thought. Future research in this direction will help to precisely identify and quantify the role of model parameters for the rAVS-CoO+ model (and the related models AVS+, AVS-BB+, and rAVS+). In addition, the Bayesian toolkit comprises several other methods for model inspection and model comparison.

Acknowledgments

This research was supported by the Cluster of Excellence Cognitive Interaction Technology 'CITEC' (EXC 277) at Bielefeld University, which is funded by the German Research Foundation (DFG).

References

Raquel G. Alhama, Remko Scha, and Willem Zuidema. 2015. How should we evaluate models of segmentation in artificial language learning? In *Proceedings of the 13th International Conference on Cognitive Modeling*.

Michele Burigo, Kenny R. Coventry, Angelo Cangelosi, and Dermot Lynott. 2016. Spatial language and converseness. *Quarterly Journal of Experimental Psychology*, 69(12):2319–2337.

Nick Chater and Christopher D Manning. 2006. Probabilistic models of language processing and acquisition. *Trends in Cognitive Sciences*, 10(7):335–344.

Kenny R. Coventry, Angelo Cangelosi, Rohanna Rajapakse, Alison Bacon, Stephen Newstead, Dan Joyce, and Lynn V. Richards. 2005. Spatial prepositions and vague quantifiers: Implementing the functional geometric framework. In *Spatial Cognition IV. Reasoning, Action, Interaction*. Springer.

Paul H. Garthwaite, Yanan Fan, and Scott A. Sisson. 2016. Adaptive optimal scaling of Metropolis–Hastings algorithms using the Robbins–Monro process. *Communications in Statistics-Theory and Methods*, 45(17):5098–5111.

Andrew Gelman and Donald B. Rubin. 1992. Inference from iterative simulation using multiple sequences. *Statistical Science*, 7(4):457–472.

Ruth Heller, Dylan Small, and Paul Rosenbaum. 2012. *crossmatch: The cross-match test*. R package version 1.3-1.

Thomas Hörberg. 2008. Influences of form and function on the acceptability of projective prepositions in Swedish. *Spatial Cognition & Computation*, 8(3):193–218.

Thomas Kluth. 2018. A C++ implementation of cognitive models of spatial language understanding as well as pertinent empirical data and analyses. will soon be published under https://pub.uni-bielefeld.de/person/54885831/data.

Thomas Kluth, Michele Burigo, and Pia Knoeferle. 2017. Modeling the directionality of attention during spatial language comprehension. In Jaap van den Herik and Joaquim Filipe, editors, *Agents and Artificial Intelligence*, Lecture Notes in Computer Science. Springer International Publishing AG.

Thomas Kluth, Michele Burigo, Holger Schultheis, and Pia Knoeferle. under revision. Does direction matter? Linguistic asymmetries reflected in visual attention. *Cognition*.

Thomas Kluth and Holger Schultheis. 2014. Attentional distribution and spatial language. In Christian Freksa, Bernhard Nebel, Mary Hegarty, and Thomas Barkowsky, editors, *Spatial Cognition IX*, Lecture Notes in Computer Science. Springer.

John K. Kruschke. 2015. *Doing Bayesian data analysis: A tutorial with R, JAGS, and Stan*, 2nd edition. Academic Press.

Jey Han Lau, Alexander Clark, and Shalom Lappin. 2017. Grammaticality, acceptability, and probability: a probabilistic view of linguistic knowledge. *Cognitive Science*, 41(5):1202–1241.

Torrin M. Liddell and John K. Kruschke. 2018. Analyzing ordinal data with metric models: What could possibly go wrong? Preprint, retrieved from osf.io/9h3et.

Gordon D. Logan and Daniel D. Sadler. 1996. A computational analysis of the apprehension of spatial relations. In Paul Bloom, Mary A. Peterson, Lynn Nadel, and Merill F. Garrett, editors, *Language and Space*, chapter 13. The MIT Press.

Xavier Fernández-i Marín. 2016. ggmcmc: Analysis of MCMC samples and Bayesian inference. *Journal of Statistical Software*, 70(9):1–20.

Daniel J. Navarro, Thomas L. Griffiths, Mark Steyvers, and Michael D. Lee. 2006. Modeling individual differences using Dirichlet processes. *Journal of Mathematical Psychology*, 50(2):101–122.

Ulrike Padó, Matthew W. Crocker, and Frank Keller. 2009. A probabilistic model of semantic plausibility in sentence processing. *Cognitive Science*, 33(5):794–838.

Terry Regier and Laura A. Carlson. 2001. Grounding spatial language in perception: An empirical and computational investigation. *Journal of Experimental Psychology: General*, 130(2):273–298.

Paul R. Rosenbaum. 2005. An exact distribution-free test comparing two multivariate distributions based on adjacency. *Journal of the Royal Statistical Society: Series B (Statistical Methodology)*, 67(4):515–530.

Conrad Sanderson and Ryan Curtin. 2016. Armadillo: a template-based C++ library for linear algebra. *Journal of Open Source Software*, 1:26.

Holger Schultheis, Ankit Singhaniya, and Devendra Singh Chaplot. 2013. Comparing model comparison methods. In *Proc. of the 35th Annual Conference of the Cognitive Science Society*, pages 1294 – 1299, Austin, TX. Cognitive Science Society.

Jon Sprouse. 2013. Acceptability judgments. In *Oxford Bibliographies*. Oxford University Press.

Brandon M. Turner and Trisha Van Zandt. 2012. A tutorial on approximate Bayesian computation. *Journal of Mathematical Psychology*, 56(2):69–85.

The Role of Syntax during Pronoun Resolution: Evidence from fMRI

Jixing Li
Department of Linguistics
Cornell University
jl2939@cornell.edu

Murielle Fabre
Department of Linguistics
Cornell University
mf684@cornell.edu

Wen-Ming Luh
Cornell MRI Facility
Cornell University
wl358@cornell.edu

John Hale
Department of Linguistics
Cornell University
jthale@cornell.edu

Abstract

The current study examined the role of syntactic structure during pronoun resolution. We correlated complexity measures derived by the syntax-sensitive Hobbs algorithm and a neural network model for pronoun resolution with brain activity of participants listening to an audiobook during fMRI recording. Compared to the neural network model, the Hobbs algorithm is associated with larger clusters of brain activation in a network including the left Broca's area.

1 Introduction

Approaching the issue of pronoun resolution from the perspectives of generative linguistics, possible antecedents for pronouns and reflexives are constrained by syntactic structures. For instance, the classical Binding Theory (Chomsky, 1981) states that reflexives are bound in their "local domain" while pronouns are not. [1] For example, "himself" in (1) has to refer to the subject of the inflectional phrase (IP) "Bill", while "him" in (2) cannot refer to "Bill".

(1) John$_i$ thinks that [$_{IP}$Bill$_j$ always criticizes himself$_{*i/j/*k}$].

(2) John$_i$ thinks that [$_{IP}$Bill$_j$ always criticizes him$_{i/*j/k}$].

Nevertheless, it is still unclear what role the binding theory play in the cognitive process of pronoun resolution. It has been argued that explicit syntactic structure and the associated parsing algorithms may not be necessary during sentence comprehension (e.g. Frank and Christiansen, 2018). Furthermore, recent neural network models of coreference resolution (e.g. Clark and Manning, 2016) achieved state-of-the-art results with no explicit syntactic information.

The current study examined the role of syntactic information during pronoun resolution by correlating a complexity measure derived by the syntax-sensitive Hobbs algorithm (Hobbs, 1977) for pronoun resolution with brain activity of participants listened to an audiobook during fMRI recoding. The Hobbs algorithm searches for the gender and number matching antecedent by traversing the parsed syntactic tree in a left-to-right, breadth-first order. We compared brain activation associated with the Hobbs algorithm to that associated with a neural network model for coreference resolution (Clark and Manning, 2016) which encodes no explicit syntactic structures. The results revealed larger clusters for the Hobbs algorithm than for the neural network model in the left Broca's area, the bilateral Angular Gyrus, the left Inferior Temporal Gyrus and the left Precuneus. Given the elements in the Hobbs algorithm including syntactic constraints and gender/number matching, we interpret these areas as supporting morpho-syntactic processing during pronoun resolution.

In the following sections, we briefly describe the Hobbs algorithm and the neural network model and compare their performance on the text of the audiobook. We then describe our linking hypotheses for correlating the models with brain activity, before presenting the methods, results and discussion of the fMRI experiment.

---

[1] A "local domain" can be roughly defined as the smallest IP or NP which contains the predicate that assigns the theta roles, the complements to which the internal theta roles are assigned, and the subject to which the external theta role is assigned.

Proceedings of the Eighth Workshop on Cognitive Aspects of Computational Language Learning and Processing, pages 56–64
Melbourne, Australia, July 19, 2018. ©2018 Association for Computational Linguistics

2 The Hobbs Algorithm

The Hobbs algorithm, originally presented in Hobbs (1977), depends only on a syntactic parser plus a morphological gender and number checker. The input to the Hobbs algorithm includes the target pronoun and the parsed trees for the current and previous sentences. The algorithm searches for a gender and number matching antecedent by traversing the tree in a left-to-right, breadth-first order, giving preference to closer antecedents. If no candidate antecedent is found in the current tree, the algorithm searches on the preceding sentence in the same order. The steps of the Hobbs algorithm are as follows:

(1) Begin at the NP node immediately dominating the pronoun.

(2) Go up the tree to the first NP or S node encountered. Call this node X, and call the path used to reach it p.

(3) Traverse all branches below node X to the left of path p in a left-to-right, breadth-first fashion. Propose as the antecedent any NP node that is encountered which has an NP or S node between it and X.

(4) If node X is the highest S node in the sentence, traverse the surface parse trees of previous sentences in the text in order of recency, the most recent first; each tree is traversed in a left-to-right, breadth-first manner, and when an NP node is encountered, it is proposed as antecedent. If X is not the highest S node in the sentence, continue to step 5.

(5) From node X, go up the tree to the first NP or S node encountered. Call this new node X, and call the path traversed to reach it p.

(6) If X is an NP node and if the path p to X did not pass through the $\bar{N}$ node that X immediately dominates, propose X as the antecedent.

(7) Traverse all branches below node X to the left of path p in a left-to-right, breadth-first manner. Propose any NP node encountered as the antecedent.

(8) If X is an S node, traverse all branches of node X to the right of path p in a left-to-right. breadth-first manner, but do not go below any NP or S node encountered. Propose any NP node encountered as the antecedent.

(9) Go to step 4.

The Hobbs algorithm conforms to the Binding Theory as it always searches for the antecedent in the left of the NP (Principle B: Step 3) and does not go below any NP or S node encountered (Principle A: Step 8). It also respects gender, person, and number agreement, and captures recency and grammatical role preferences in the order it performs the search. Hobbs (1977) evaluated his algorithm on 300 examples containing third person pronouns, and it worked in 88.3% of the cases. With some selectional constraints on dates and location antecedents (i.e., restricting dates and location NPs such as "2018" and "school" to be the antecedent of "it"), the algorithm achieved 91.7% accuracy. However, the test dataset was limited in size and the performance degraded when there were competing antecedents. We propose here to test its accuracy on a larger dataset including 1499 sentences with 465 third person pronouns.

3 The Neural Network Model

The neural network model for pronoun resolution is adapted from the neural network model for both pronominal and nominal coreference resolution (Clark and Manning, 2016). This model consists of a *mention-pair encoder*, a *cluster-pair encoder*, a *mention-ranking model* and a *cluster-ranking model*. The *mention-pair encoder* generates distributed representations for pronoun-antecedent pairs, or mention pairs, by passing relevant features through a feed-forward neural network. The *cluster-pair encoder* generates distributed representations for pairs of clusters through a pooling operation over representations of relevant mention pairs. The *mention-ranking model* scores the candidate antecedents to prune the set of possible antecedent and the *cluster-ranking model* scores coreference compatibility for each pair of clusters.

The input layer of the neural network model consists of a large set of features including word embeddings for the mention pairs, type and length of the mentions, linear distance between the mention pairs, etc. (see Table 1). These feature vectors are concatenated to produce an I-dimensional vector $h_0(a, m)$ as the representation for the mention m and the antecedent a. The input layer then passes through three hidden layers of rectified linear units (ReLU), and the output of the last hidden layer is the vector representation for the mention pair $r_m(a, m)$.

$$h_i(a, m) = ReLU(W_i h_{i-1}(a, m) + b_i)$$

For pairs of clusters $c_i = \{m_1^i, m_2^i, ..., m_{c_i}^i\}$ and $c_j = \{m_1^j, m_2^j, ..., m_{c_j}^j\}$, the *cluster-pair encoder* first forms a matrix $R_m(c_i, c_j) = [r_m(m_1^i, m_1^j), r_m(m_2^i, m_2^j), ..., r_m(m_{c_i}^i, m_{c_j}^j)]$, then applies a pooling operation over $R_m(c_i, c_j)$ to produce a distributed representation for the cluster pair $r_c(c_i, c_j)$. The *mention-ranking model* assigns a score for each mention pair by applying a single fully connected layer of size one the mention pair representation $r_m(a, m)$. The model is then trained with the max-margin training objective.

$$s_m(a, m) = W_m r_m(a, m) + b_m$$

Similarly, the *cluster-ranking model* assigns a coreference score for each cluster pair and an anaphoricity score for mention m (i.e., how likely mention m has an antecedent). These scores are used to decide whether mention m should be merged with one preceding cluster or not during testing.

$$s_c(c_i, c_j) = W_c r_c(c_i, c_j) + b_c$$

$$s_{NA}(m) = W_{NA} r_m(NA, m) + b_{NA}$$

Feature Type	Description
Word embedding	head word
	dependency parent
	first word
	last word
	two preceding words
	two following words
	averaged of the five preceding words
	averaged of five following words
	all words in the mention
	all words in the mention's sentence
	and all words in the mention's document
Mention	type (pronoun/noun/proper name/list)
	position in the document
	contained in another mention or not
	length of the mention in words
Document	genre (broadcast news/newswire/web data)
Distance	intervening sentences
	number intervening mentions
	mentions overlap or not
String matching	head match
	exact string match
	partial string match

Table 1: *Feature set of the neural network model (Clark and Manning, 2016).*

The neural network model encodes no explicit syntactic structures, but it captures semantic information in its word embedding features. It also incorporates discourse-level information such as linear distance between the mention pairs across several sentences, discourse genre, etc. Clark and Manning (2016) trained the model on the CoNLL-2012 Shared Task (Pradhan et al., 2012) and it achieved state-of-the-art results in both the English and Chinese test set.

The neural network model was evaluated on both pronominal and nominal coreference resolution, however, pronouns and full noun phrases (NPs) may rely on very different set of features. For example, string matching and measures for semantic similarity are powerful features for nominal coreference resolution, but are not applicable for pronoun resolution as word embeddings do not represent pronouns well. In addition, it has been argued that pronouns serve a different discourse function from that of full NPs in that full NPs introduce new entities in the discourse and pronouns maintain the reference (Sanford et al., 1988). Based on these arguments, it is reasonable to say that pronoun resolution and full NP coreference involves different cognitive processes.

4 Evaluating the Models on Text Data

4.1 Text Data

The text data is an English audiobook version of Antoine de Saint-Exupéry's *The Little Prince*. Within the audiobook text, 1755 pronouns and 3127 non-pronominal entities (4882 mentions in total) are identified using the annotation tool brat (Stenetorp et al., 2012; see Figure 1). Reflexives (e.g., "herself") and possessives (e.g., "his") are excluded from the dataset as they have different "binding domains" from pronouns according to the Binding Theory and hence influences performance of the Hobbs algorithm. Pronouns with sentential antecedents (e.g, the second "it" in the conversation "That is funny where you live a day only last a minute." "It is not funny at all."), as well as dummy pronouns (e.g., "it" in "It said in the book that ...") are also removed. The resulting dataset contains 645 first person pronouns, 302 second person pronouns and 675 third person pronouns (see Table 2).

1st	i	me	we	us
	505	121	16	3
2nd	you			
	302			
3rd	she	her	he	him
	41	14	268	64
	it	they	them	
	136	94	58	

Table 2: Attestations of each pronoun type in *The Little Prince.*

We decided to focus only on the third person pronouns because they provide gender and number information that feeds the Hobbs algorithm. In addition, third person pronouns have been suggested to differ from first and second person pronouns in that first and second person pronouns mark proximity in space and third person pronouns are further away (Ariel, 1990). Therefore, we further excluded third person pronouns whose antecedents

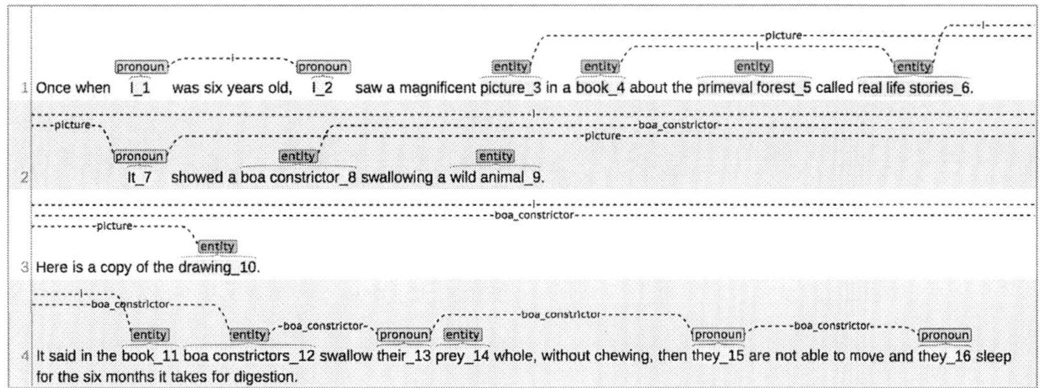

Figure 1: Sample annotations of pronouns and non-pronoun mentions in English, visualized using the annotation tool brat (Stenetorp et al., 2012).

are first and second person pronouns. The final test set contains 465 third person pronouns.

4.2 Model Performance

To evaluate performance of the Hobbs algorithm and the neural network model for third person pronoun resolution in *The Little Prince*, we compared the predicted antecedents for the 465 third person pronouns with the correct immediate antecedents. We considers only the immediate antecedent as the Hobbs algorithm only propose one antecedent and does not group the proposed antecedent into clusters. The syntactic trees for the sentences in the text are parsed by the Stanford PCFG parser (Klein and Manning, 2003).

For the neural network model, we used the pretrained weights from Clark and Manning (2016) to output a coreference score for all the potential pronoun-antecedent pairs. If the score of the immediate antecedent ranks among top three of all the candidate antecedents, the prediction is marked as correct.

Table 3 shows the accuracy of the Hobbs algorithm and the neural network model for third person pronouns in *The Little Prince*. The neural coreference model only achieves a 0.4 accuracy. Compared with the high F1 score (0.74) for pronoun and full NP coreference resolution on the CoNLL-2012 English test data (Clark and Manning, 2016), this low accuracy confirmed that pronominal and nominal coreference resolution rely on different feature sets. String matching and semantic similarity, for example, may be less powerful for pronominal resolution.

On the other hand, the Hobbs algorithm identi-fies the correct immediate antecedent for 60% of the third person pronouns. Given the elements of the Hobbs algorithm, it is suggested that linguistically motivated features, especially syntactic constraints and gender/number cues, may be more relevant for third person pronoun resolution in English.

	Accuracy
Hobbs Algorithm	0.60
Neural Network	0.40

Table 3: Performance of the Hobbs algorithm and the neural network model on third pronoun resolution in *The Little Prince*.

4.3 Error Analysis

To probe why the neural network model performed relatively poor than the Hobbs algorithm for third person pronoun resolution, we further divided the dataset into "same sentence" and "different sentence" conditions depending on whether the antecedent occurs within the same sentence of the pronoun. 155 of the 465 third person pronouns have antecedents in the same sentence. Table 4 lists the accuracy of the two models in the two conditions. It can be seen that the Hobbs algorithm performs equally well for the same and different sentence conditions, whereas the neural network model performs worse if the antecedent is not in the same sentence as the pronoun.

A closer examination on the wrong 279 cases predicted by the neural network model revealed that the model tends to be misled by the "partial string match" feature, such that it gives high coref-

	Hobbs	**Neural Network**
Same Sentence	0.60	0.50
Different Sentence	0.60	0.35

Table 4: Accuracy of the Hobbs algorithm and the neural network model for third person pronouns that have antecedents in the same or different sentences.

erence scores for "that" and "they". This confirmed our hypothesis that pronominal and nominal coreference resolution rely on different set of features.

5 Correlating Model Prediction with Brain Activity

5.1 Linking Hypotheses

To explain how the model performance are specifically brought to bear on brain activity, we further correlated activation levels of the antecedents with fMRI time-courses when participants listened to *The Little Prince* in the scanner.

We first selected the 277 third person pronouns whose antecedents are correctly predicted by the Hobbs algorithm, i.e., the true positives, and we calculated the Hobbs distance for each of the 277 pronouns, namely, the number of NPs that the Hobbs algorithm skips before the antecedent NP is proposed. Our linking hypotheses is that a higher Hobbs distance induces a processing effort for pronoun resolution, hence higher hemodynamic response.

Note that the Hobbs distance is different from the number of NP nodes between the pronoun and the antecedents, as the Hobbs algorithm always searches the antecedent to the left of the pronoun in a left-to-right, breadth-first order. Figure 2 shows the Hobbs distance for the two "they" in the example sentence. The immediate antecedent for "they_1" is "their", and the Hobbs distance between "their" and "they_1" is 2 because the algorithm skips the NP "boa constrictors" before proposes "their" as the antecedent. The Hobbs distance for "they_2" is 1 because the correct antecedent is the first proposal by the algorithm.

In comparison, we recorded the coreference score $S_m(a, m)$ generated by the neural network model for the 277 pronouns that correctly predicted by the Hobbs algorithm. We took the negative of the score as a complexity measure for the neural coreference model: the higher the score,

the more difficult to retrieve the antecedent. Pearson's r revealed no significant correlation between the Hobbs distance and the negative neural coreference score for the 227 third person pronouns ($r = 0.05, p = 0.43$).

5.2 Predicted Brain Activation

Based on the elements in the Hobbs algorithm and the neural network model, we expected the difficulty of pronoun resolution modeled by the Hobbs distance and the neural coreference score to tease apart brain areas that are associated with syntactic and morphological processing, and brain areas that are sensitive to semantic and discourse-level information.

Previous neuroimaging results on pronoun resolution have reported the bilateral Inferior Frontal Gyrus (IFG), the left Medial Frontal Gyrus (MFG) and the bilateral Supramarginal/Angular Gyrus in gender mismatch between pronoun and antecedent (Hammer et al., 2007). We therefore expect activity in these regions for the Hobbs distance metric. We also expect to see activity in the bilateral Superior Temporal Gyrus (STGs) as they have been associated with long distance pronoun-antecedent linking (Matchin et al., 2014). These regions could be relevant for both the Hobbs distance and neural coreference score as they both incorporate some form of "distance" between the pronoun-antecedent pairs. The Precuneus cortex may also be activated with pronouns in general as it has been suggested to track different sorts of story characters (Wehbe et al., 2014).

6 Brain Data

6.1 Participants

Participants were 49 healthy, right-handed, young adults (30 female, mean age = 21.3, range = 18-37). They self-identified as native English speakers, and had no history of psychiatric, neurological or other medical illness that could compromise cognitive functions. All participants were paid for, and gave written informed consent prior to participation, in accordance with the guidelines of the Human Research Participant Protection Program at Cornell University.

6.2 Stimuli

The stimulus was an audiobook version of Antoine de Saint-Exupéry's *The Little Prince*, translated

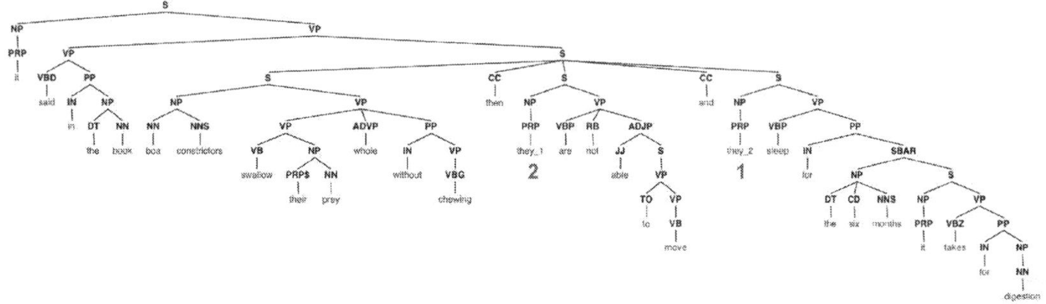

Figure 2: Demonstration of Hobbs distance for third person pronouns in a sentence. The red numbers below the pronouns indicates the Hobbs distance.

by David Wilkinson and read by Nadine Eckert-Boulet. This text contains 3127 non-pronominal mentions and 645 first person pronouns, 302 second person pronouns and 675 third person pronouns (see Table 2). Following the pruning criteria described in Section 5, the final set of data include 277 third person pronouns.

6.3 Procedure

After giving their informed consent, participants were familiarized with the MRI facility and assumed a supine position on the scanner. The presentation script was written in PsychoPy (Peirce, 2007). Auditory stimuli were delivered through MRI-safe, high-fidelity headphones (Confon HP-VS01, MR Confon, Magdeburg, Germany) inside the head coil. The headphones were secured against the plastic frame of the coil using foam blocks. An experimenter increased the sound volume stepwise until the participants could hear clearly.

The audiobook lasts for about 94 minutes, and was divided into nine sections, each lasts for about ten minutes. Participants listened passively to the nine sections and completed four quiz questions after each section (36 questions in total). These questions were used to confirm their comprehension and were viewed by the participants via a mirror attached to the head coil and they answered through a button box. The entire session lasted around 2.5 hours.

6.4 MRI Data Collection and Preprocessing

The brain imaging data were acquired with a 3T MRI GE Discovery MR750 scanner with a 32-channel head coil. Anatomical scans were acquired using a T1-weighted volumetric Magnetization Prepared RApid Gradient-Echo (MP-RAGE) pulse sequence. Blood-oxygen-level-dependent (BOLD) functional scans were acquired using a multi-echo planar imaging (ME-EPI) sequence with online reconstruction (TR=2000 ms; TE's=12.8, 27.5, 43 ms; FA=77°; matrix size=72 x 72; FOV=240.0 mm x 240.0 mm; 2 x image acceleration; 33 axial slices, voxel size=3.75 x 3.75 x 3.8 mm). Cushions and clamps were used to minimize head movement during scanning.

All fMRI data is preprocessed using AFNI version 16 (Cox, 1996). The first 4 volumes in each run were excluded from analyses to allow for T1-equilibration effects. Multi-echo independent components analysis (ME-ICA; Kundu et al.,2012) were used to denoise data for motion, physiology and scanner artifacts. Images were then spatially normalized to the standard space of the Montreal Neurological Institute (MNI) atlas, yielding a volumetric time series resampled at 2 mm cubic voxels.

6.5 Statistical Analysis

At the single subject level, the observed BOLD time course in each voxel were modeled by the difficulty of pronoun resolution derived by the Hobbs Algorithm and the Neural Network Model for third person pronouns time-locked at the offset of each third person pronoun in the audiobook. To further examine the status of Hobbs and Neural Network Models as cognitive models for pronoun resolution, we also included a binary regressor that simply marks the presence of a third person pronoun time-locked at the offset of each third person pronoun in the audiobook.

In addition, three control variables of non-theoretical interest were included in the GLM analysis: *RMS intensity* at every 10 ms of the audio; *word rate* at the offset of each spoken word in time; *frequency* of the individual words in Google Book unigrams [2]. These regressors were added to ensure that any conclusions about pronoun resolution would be specific to those processes, as opposed to more general aspects of speech perception.

At the group level, the activation maps for the Hobbs, neural network and binary regressor were computed using one sample t-test. The voxelwise threshold was set at $p \leq 0.05\ FWE$, with an extent threshold of 50 contiguous voxels ($k \geq 50$).

7   fMRI Results

The largest clusters for the binary third person pronoun regressor were observed in the bilateral Superior Temporal Gyrus (STGs), the left Inferior Frontal Gyrus (IFG), the left Superior Frontal Gyrus (STG), the right Cerebellum and the right Angular Gyrus ($p < 0.05\ FWE$; see Figure 3a).

Hobbs algorithm shows significant activation in the left Precuneus, the bilateral Angular Gyrus, the left IFG and the left SFG ($p < 0.05\ FWE$; see Figure 3b). For the neural network model, although the cluster size is relatively small at the corrected threshold, it has significant clusters in the right STG and the left Middle Temporal Gyrus (MTG; $p < 0.05\ FWE$; see Figure 3c). Table 5 lists all the significant clusters using region names from the Harvard-Oxford Cortical Structure Atlas.

8   Discussion

Activation map for third person pronoun resolution modeled by the Hobbs distance is a subset of the activation map for the binary third person pronoun regressor. Additional activity is observed in the Precuneus for the Hobbs regressor, suggesting that the Precuneus is involved in the process of pronoun-antecedent linking, consistent with Wehbe et al.'s (2014) finding that the Precuneus tracks the characters in a story.

Only the Hobbs algorithm showed an increased activation in the left Broca's area, which has been recurrently reported as correlating with syntactic processing cost linked to antecedent pronoun (Santi and Grodzinsky, 2012), and particularly to the distance between the antecedent and the pronoun (Matchin et al., 2014; Santi and Grodzinsky, 2007).

The bilateral Angular Gyrus activity was also significant for the Hobbs algorithm. Notably, previous literature on German gender agreement in anaphoric reference reported increased activation in the left Angular Gyrus (BA 39) for incongruent biological gender matching (Hammer et al., 2007). Our results supported the role of morphosyntactic processing for gender matching during pronoun resolution at the Angular Gyrus.

The neural network model encodes different brain activity patterns at the right STG and the left MTG, although the cluster size is relatively small at the corrected threshold. The right STG has been reported to encode linear distance between pronouns and antecedents (Hammer et al., 2007, 2011) and for long distance back anaphora compared to short-distance back anaphora (Matchin et al., 2014). The MTGs have been associated with intra-sentential co-referential link (Fabre, 2017). This is expected as the neural network model encodes the linear distance between the pronoun and the antecedent. The MTGs were also reported to respond to highly predictive lexical access (Fruchter et al., 2015), suggesting that difficulty of pronoun resolution modeled by the neural network scores is likely to involve lexical semantic processing.

9   Conclusion

Comparison of model performance between the Hobbs algorithm and the neural network model on pronoun resolution suggest an important role for syntactic and morphological cues during pronoun resolution. These two types of information were integrated in the Hobbs distance measure that reflects processing difficulty of pronoun resolution. This difficulty measure is associated with significant activity in the left Broca's area, the bilateral Angular Gyrus and the left IFG — a network that has been reported in the neuroimaging literature for anaphora resolution.

Overall, our results show that crossing computational approach and naturalistic stimuli is a promising perspective in neuroimaging to tease apart strongly interwoven cognitive processes. As such, they pave the way for increasing cross-fertilization between computational linguistics and the cognitive neuroscience of language.

---

[2] http://books.google.com/ngrams

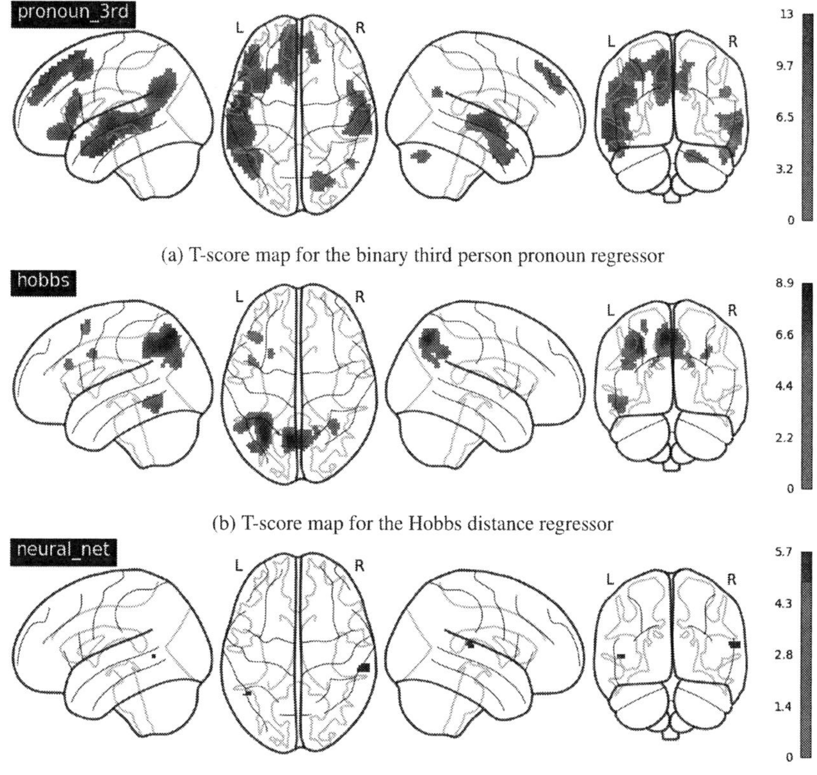

(a) T-score map for the binary third person pronoun regressor

(b) T-score map for the Hobbs distance regressor

(c) T-score map for the negative neural network score regressor

Figure 3: Whole-brain effect with significant clusters for (a) binary third person pronouns effect, (b) difficulty for third pronoun resolution based on the Hobbs algorithm and (c) difficulty for third person pronoun resolution based on the neural coreference model. All images underwent *FWE* voxel correction for multiple comparisons with p < 0.05.

| | MNI coordinates | | | Region | p-value | k-size | t-score |
	x	y	z		*FWE-corr*	*cluster*	*peak*
Third Person Pronoun	-60	-12	-6	left Superior Temporal Gyrus	< 0.001	4411	12.92
(binary)	64	-10	-2	right Superior Temporal Gyrus	< 0.001	1625	10.95
	-46	30	-12	left Inferior Frontal Gyrus	< 0.001	706	10.53
	-10	42	46	left Superior Frontal Gyrus	< 0.001	2394	10.45
	18	-74	-30	right Cerebellum	< 0.001	283	7.15
	52	-60	26	right Angular Gyrus	0.004	68	5.84
Hobbs Algorithm	-6	-68	50	left Precuneus	< 0.001	1163	8.86
	-32	-62	42	left Angular Gyrus	< 0.001	1216	8.42
	-52	-56	-16	left Inferior Temporal Gyrus	< 0.001	285	6.54
	34	-52	34	right Angular Gyrus	0.001	119	6.31
	-44	6	34	left Inferior Frontal Gyrus	0.005	55	5.01
	-26	12	60	left Superior Frontal Gyrus	0.007	62	5.63
Neural Network	62	-28	14	right Superior Temporal Gyrus	0.005	48	5.69
	-46	-54	4	left Middle Temporal Gyrus	0.008	13	5.55

Table 5: Significant clusters of BOLD activation for (a) third person pronouns, (b) difficulty for third person pronoun resolution based on the Hobbs algorithm and (c) difficulty for third person pronoun resolution based on the neural coreference model. Peak activations are given in MNI Coordinates ($p <$ 0.05, *FWE*).

Acknowledgments

This material is based upon work supported by the National Science Foundation under Grant No.1607441.

References

M. Ariel. 1990. *Accessing noun-phrase antecedents*. Routledge, London, UK.

Noam Chomsky. 1981. *Lectures on government and binding*. Foris, Dordrecht, Holland.

Kevin Clark and Christopher D. Manning. 2016. Improving coreference resolution by learning entity-level distributed representations. *arXiv:1606.01323*.

R. W. Cox. 1996. AFNI: software for analysis and visualization of functional magnetic resonance neuroimages. *Computers and Biomedical Research, an International Journal*, 29(3):162–173.

Murielle Fabre. 2017. *The sentence as cognitive object - The neural underpinnings of syntactic complexity in Chinese and French*. Ph.D. thesis, INALCO Paris.

Stefan L. Frank and Morten H. Christiansen. 2018. Hierarchical and sequential processing of language: A response to: Ding, Melloni, Tian, and Poeppel (2017). Rule-based and word-level statistics-based processing of language: insights from neuroscience. *Language, Cognition and Neuroscience . Language, Cognition and Neuroscience*, pages 1–6.

Joseph Fruchter, Tal Linzen, Masha Westerlund, and Alec Marantz. 2015. Lexical Preactivation in Basic Linguistic Phrases. *Journal of Cognitive Neuroscience*, 27(10):1912–1935.

Anke Hammer, Rainer Goebel, Jens Schwarzbach, Thomas F. Münte, and Bernadette M. Jansma. 2007. When sex meets syntactic gender on a neural basis during pronoun processing. *Brain Research*, 1146:185–198.

Anke Hammer, Bernadette M. Jansma, Claus Tempelmann, and Thomas F. Münte. 2011. Neural mechanisms of anaphoric reference revealed by fMRI. *Frontiers in Psychology*, 2.

Jerry Hobbs. 1977. Resolving pronouns. In *Readings in natural language processing*. Morgan Kaufman Publishers, Inc., Los Altos, California, USA.

D. Klein and C. Manning. 2003. Accurate unlexicalized parsing. In *Proceedings of the 41st Meeting of the association for computational linguistics.*, pages 423–430.

Prantik Kundu, Souheil J. Inati, Jennifer W. Evans, Wen-Ming Luh, and Peter A. Bandettini. 2012. Differentiating BOLD and non-BOLD signals in fMRI time series using multi-echo EPI. *NeuroImage*, 60(3):1759–1770.

William Matchin, Jon Sprouse, and Gregory Hickok. 2014. A structural distance effect for backward anaphora in Broca's area: An fMRI study. *Brain and Language*, 138:1–11.

Jonathan W. Peirce. 2007. PsychoPy—Psychophysics software in Python. *Journal of Neuroscience Methods*, 162(1-2):8–13.

Sameer Pradhan, Alessandro Moschitti, Nianwen Xue, Olga Uryupina, and Yuchen Zhang. 2012. CoNLL-2012 shared task: Modeling multilingual unrestricted coreference in OntoNotes. In *Proceedings of the Sixteenth Conference on Computational Natural Language Learning (CoNLL 2012)*, Jeju, Korea.

Anthony J. Sanford, K. Moar, and Simon C. Garrod. 1988. Proper names as controllers of discourse focus. *Language and speech*, 31(1):43–56.

Andrea Santi and Yosef Grodzinsky. 2007. Taxing working memory with syntax: Bihemispheric modulations. *Human Brain Mapping*, 28(11):1089–1097.

Andrea Santi and Yosef Grodzinsky. 2012. Broca's area and sentence comprehension: A relationship parasitic on dependency, displacement or predictability? *Neuropsychologia*, 50(5):821–832.

Pontus Stenetorp, Sampo Pyysalo, Goran Topić, Tomoko Ohta, Sophia Ananiadou, and Jun'ichi Tsujii. 2012. BRAT: a web-based tool for NLP-assisted text annotation. In *Proceedings of the Demonstrations at the 13th Conference of the European Chapter of the Association for Computational Linguistics*, pages 102–107. Association for Computational Linguistics.

Leila Wehbe, Ashish Vaswani, Kevin Knight, and Tom M. Mitchell. 2014. Aligning context-based statistical models of language with brain activity during reading. In *EMNLP*, pages 233–243.

A Sound and Complete Left-Corner Parsing for Minimalist Grammars

Miloš Stanojević
University of Edinburgh
Edinburgh EH8 9AB, UK
m.stanojevic@ed.ac.uk

Edward P. Stabler
UCLA and Nuance Communications
California, USA
edward.stabler@nuance.com

Abstract

This paper presents a left-corner parser for minimalist grammars. The relation between the parser and the grammar is transparent in the sense that there is a very simple 1-1 correspondence between derivations and parses. Like left-corner context-free parsers, left-corner minimalist parsers can be non-terminating when the grammar has empty left corners, so an easily computed left-corner oracle is defined to restrict the search.

1 Introduction

Minimalist grammars (MGs) (Stabler, 1997) were inspired by proposals in Chomskian syntax (Chomsky, 1995). MGs are strictly more expressive than context free grammars (CFGs) and weakly equivalent to multiple context free grammars (MCFGs) (Michaelis, 2001; Harkema, 2001a). The literature presents bottom-up and top-down parsers for MGs (Harkema, 2001b), which differ in the order in which derivations are constructed, and consequently they may differ in their memory demands at each point in the parse. But partly because of those memory demands, parsers that mix top-down and bottom-up steps are often regarded as psycholinguistically more plausible (Hale, 2014; Resnik, 1992; Abney and Johnson, 1991).

Among mixed strategies, left-corner parsing (LC) is perhaps the best known (Rosenkrantz and Lewis, 1970). A left-corner parser does not begin by guessing what's in the string, as a top-down parser does. But it also does not just reduce elements of the input, as a bottom-up parser does. A left-corner parser looks first at what is in the string (completing the left-most constituent, bottom-up) and then predicting the

sisters of that element (top-down), if any. The following CFG trees have nodes numbered in the order they would be constructed by bottom-up, left-corner and top-down strategies:

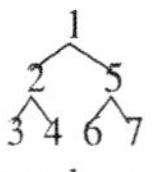 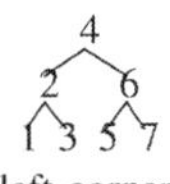 

top-down   left-corner   bottom-up

LC parsing is bottom-up on the leftmost leaf, but then proposes a completed parent of that node on condition that its predicted sister is found.

For CFGs, LC parsing is well understood (Aho and Ullman, 1972; Rosenkrantz and Lewis, 1970). In a CF rule $A \rightarrow B\ C$, the left corner is of course always B. Johnson and Roark (2000) generalize from CFGs to unification-based grammars and show how to allow some selected categories to be parsed left-corner while others are parsed top-down. Extending these ideas to MGs, we must deal with movements, with rules that sometimes have their first daughter on the left and sometimes on the right, and with categories that are sometimes empty and sometimes not. Left corner parsers were developed for some other discontinuous formalisms with similar properties (van Noord, 1991; Díaz et al., 2002) but in all cases these parsers fall in the category of the arc-standard left corner parsing. Here we present a left corner parser that is of arc-eager type which is argued to be more cognitively plausible due to its higher degree of incrementality (Abney and Johnson, 1991; Resnik, 1992).

A first approach to left-corner MG parsing, designed to involve a kind of psycholinguistically motivated search, has been presented (Hunter, 2017), but that proposal does not handle all MGs. In particular, remnant movement presents the main challenge to Hunter's parser. The parser proposed here handles all MGs, and it is easily shown to be sound and complete via a simple 1-1 correspon-

Proceedings of the Eighth Workshop on Cognitive Aspects of Computational Language Learning and Processing, pages 65–74
Melbourne, Australia, July 19, 2018. ©2018 Association for Computational Linguistics

dence between derivations and parses. (However, as mentioned in the conclusion, the present proposal does not yet address the psycholinguistic issues raised by Hunter.) Following similar work on CFGs (Pereira and Shieber, 1987, §6.3.1), we show how to compute a left-corner oracle that can improve efficiency. And probabilities can be used in a LC beam-parser to pursue the most probable parses at each step (Manning and Carpenter, 1997).

2   Minimalist grammars

We present a succinct definition adapted from Stabler (2011, §A.1) and then consider a simple example derivation in Figure 1. An MG $G=\langle \Sigma, B, Lex, C, \{\text{merge,move}\}\rangle$, where Σ is the **vocabulary**, B is a set of **basic features**, Lex is a finite **lexicon** (as defined just below), $C \in B$ is the **start category**, and {merge,move} are the generating functions. The basic features of the set B are concatenated with prefix operators to specify their roles, as follows:

    categories, selectees $= B$

        selectors $= \{\text{=f} \,|\, \text{f} \in B\}$

        licensees $= \{\text{-f} \,|\, \text{f} \in B\}$

        licensors $= \{\text{+f} \,|\, \text{f} \in B\}$.

Let F be the set of role-marked **features**, that is, the union of the categories, selectors, licensors and licensees. Let $T=\{::, :\}$ be two **types**, indicating 'lexical' and 'derived' structures, respectively. Let $\mathbb{C} = \Sigma^* \times T \times F^*$ be the set of **chains**. Let $E = \mathbb{C}^+$ be the set of **expressions**. An expression is a chain together with its 'moving' sub-chains, if any. Then the **lexicon** $Lex \subset \Sigma^* \times \{::\} \times F^*$ is a finite set. We write ϵ for the empty string. Merge and move are defined in Table 1. Note that each merge rule deletes a selection feature =f and a corresponding category feature f, so the result on the left side of the rule has 2 features less than the total number of features on the right. Similarly, each move rule deletes a licensor feature +f and a licensee feature -f. Note also that the rules have pairwise disjoint domains; that is, an instance of a right side of a rule is not an instance of the right side of any other rule. The set of **structures**, everything you can derive from the lexicon using the rules, S(G)=closure(Lex,{merge,move}). The **sentences L(G)** $= \{s \,|\, s \cdot C \in$ S(G) for some type $\cdot \in \{:, ::\}\}$, where C is the 'start' category.

Example grammar **G1** with start category c uses features +wh and -wh to trigger wh-movements:

ϵ :: =v c	knows :: =c =d v
ϵ :: =v +wh c	likes :: =d =d v
Aca :: d	what :: d -wh
Bibi :: d	

These 7 lexical items define an infinite language. An example derivation is shown in Figure 1.

Grammar G1 is simple in a way that can be misleading, since the mechanisms that allow simple wh-movement also allow remnant movements, that is, movements of a constituent out of which something has already moved. Without remnant movements, MGs only define context-free languages (Kobele, 2010). So remnant movements are responsible for deriving copying and other sorts of crossing dependencies that cannot be enforced in a CFG. Consider **G2**:

$\bot$ :: T -r -l	$\top$ :: =T +r +l T
a :: =A +l T -l	a :: =T +r A -r
b :: =B +l T -l	b :: =T +r B -r

With T as the start category, this grammar defines the copy language $\bot XX\top$ where X is any string of a's and b's. Bracketing the reduplicated string with $\bot$ and $\top$ allows this very simple grammar with no empty categories, and makes it easy to track how the positions of these elements is defined by the derivation tree on the left in Figure 2, with 6 movements numbered 0 to 4, with TP(0) moving twice.

This example shows that simple mechanisms and simple lexical features can produce surprising patterns. Some copy-like patterns are fairly easy to see in human languages (Bresnan et al., 1982; Shieber, 1985), and many proposals with remnant derivations have become quite prominent in syntactic theory, even where copy-like patterns are not immediately obvious (den Besten and Webelhuth, 1990; Kayne, 1994; Koopman and Szabolcsi, 2000; Hinterhölzl, 2006; Grewendorf, 2015; Thoms and Walkden, 2018). Since remnant-movement analyses seem appropriate for some constructions in human languages, and since grammars defining those analyses are often quite simple, and since at least in many cases, remnant analyses are easy to compute, it would be a mistake to dismiss these derivations too quickly. For present purposes, the relevant and obvious point is that a sound and complete left corner parser for MGs must handle all such derivations.

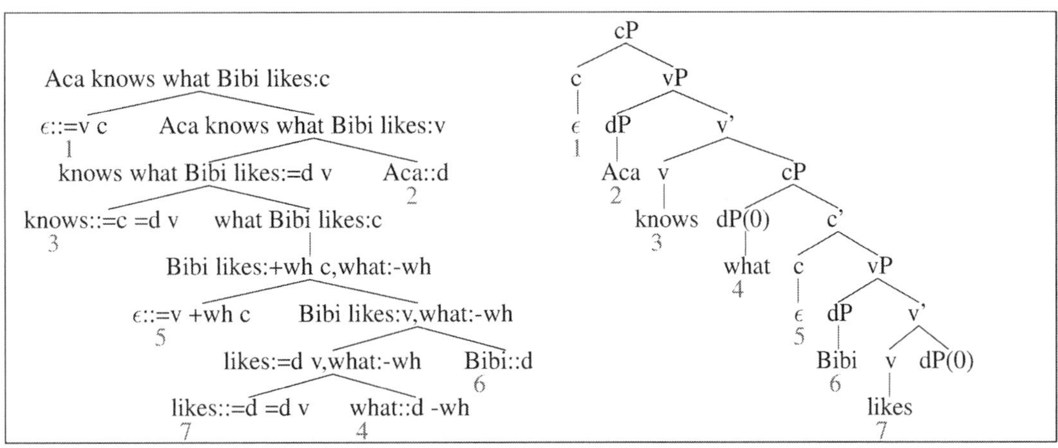

Figure 1: **Derivation tree** from **G1** on the left, and corresponding X-bar **derived tree** on the right. In the derivation tree, the binary internal nodes are applications of merge rules, while the unary node is an application of move1. Computing the derived X-bar structure from the derivation is briefly described in §5 below. Note that in the X-bar tree, P is added to each category feature when the complex is the 'maximal projection' of the head, while primes indicate intermediate projections, and the moved constituent is 'coindexed' with its origin by marking both positions with (0). For the LC parser, the derivation tree (not the derived X-bar tree) is the important object, since the derivation is what shows whether a string is derived by the grammar. But which daughter is 'leftmost' in the derivation tree is determined by the derived string positions, counted here from 1 to 7, left to right. Derived categories become left corners when they are completed, so for the nodes in the derivation tree, the leftmost daughter, in the sense relevant for LC parsing, is the one that is completed first in the left-to-right parse of the derived string.

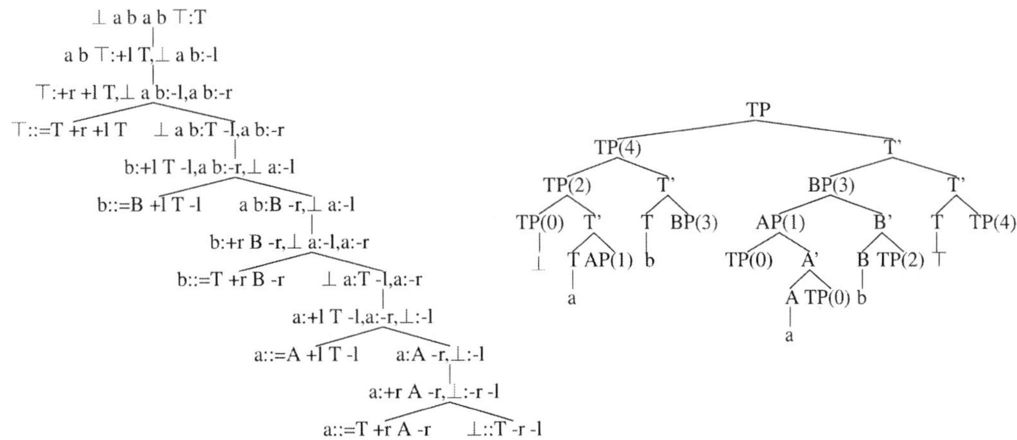

Figure 2: **Derivation tree** from **G2** on the left, and corresponding **derived tree** on the right. Note that the empty TP(0) moves twice, first with MOVE2 and then landing with MOVE1. That TP is just the empty head, the only element of G2 with 2 licensees. Graf et al. (2016) show that all MG languages can be defined without moving any phrase more than once, but G2 is beautifully small and symmetric.

$$\boxed{\begin{array}{l}
\textbf{merge} \text{ is the union of the following 3 rules, each with 2 elements on the right,} \\
\text{for strings } s, t \in \Sigma^*, \text{ for types } \cdot \in \{:, ::\} \text{ (lexical and derived, respectively),} \\
\text{for feature sequences } \gamma \in F^*, \delta \in F^+, \text{ and for chains } \alpha_1, \ldots, \alpha_k, \iota_1, \ldots, \iota_l \ (0 \leq k, l)
\end{array}}$$

(MERGE1) lexical item s selects non-mover t to produce the merged st
$$st : \gamma, \alpha_1, \ldots, \alpha_k \quad \leftarrow \quad s :: {=}f\gamma \quad t \cdot f, \alpha_1, \ldots, \alpha_k$$

(MERGE2) derived item s selects a non-mover t to produce the merged ts
$$ts : \gamma, \alpha_1, \ldots, \alpha_k, \iota_1, \ldots, \iota_l \quad \leftarrow \quad s : {=}f\gamma, \alpha_1, \ldots, \alpha_k \quad t \cdot f, \iota_1, \ldots, \iota_l$$

(MERGE3) any item s selects a mover t to produce the merged s with chain t
$$s : \gamma, \alpha_1, \ldots, \alpha_k, t : \delta, \iota_1, \ldots, \iota_l \quad \leftarrow \quad s \cdot {=}f\gamma, \alpha_1, \ldots, \alpha_k \quad t \cdot f\delta, \iota_1, \ldots, \iota_l$$

$\textbf{move}$ is the union of the following 2 rules, each with 1 element on the right, for $\delta \in F^+$, such that none of the chains $\alpha_1, \ldots, \alpha_{i-1}, \alpha_{i+1}, \ldots, \alpha_k$ has $-f$ as its first feature:

(MOVE1) final move of t, so its $-f$ chain is eliminated on the left
$$ts : \gamma, \alpha_1, \ldots, \alpha_{i-1}, \alpha_{i+1}, \ldots, \alpha_k \quad \leftarrow \quad s : {+}f\gamma, \alpha_1, \ldots, \alpha_{i-1}, t : {-}f, \alpha_{i+1}, \ldots, \alpha_k$$

(MOVE2) nonfinal move of t, so its chain continues with features δ
$$s : \gamma, \alpha_1, \ldots, \alpha_{i-1}, t : \delta, \alpha_{i+1}, \ldots, \alpha_k \quad \leftarrow \quad s : {+}f\gamma, \alpha_1, \ldots, \alpha_{i-1}, t : {-}f\delta, \alpha_{i+1}, \ldots, \alpha_k$$

Table 1: **Rules for minimalist grammars** from (Stabler, 2011, §A.1). Where a CFG has $\rightarrow$, these rules have $\leftarrow$ as a reminder that they are usually used 'bottom-up', as functions from the elements on their right sides to the corresponding value on the left. To handle movements, MGs show the strings s, t explicitly. And where CFG rules have categories, these rules have complexes, i.e. comma-separated chains. Intuitively, each chain is a string with a type and syntactic features, and each constituent on either side of these rules is a sequence of chains, an initial head chain possibly followed by moving chains.

3   Left corner MG parsing

A left corner parser uses an MG rule when the leftmost element on the right side is complete, where by leftmost element we do not mean the one that appears first in the rules of Table 1. Rather, the leftmost element is the one that is completed first in the left-to-right parse. For MOVE rules, there is just one element on the right side, so that element is the left-corner. When the right side of a MOVE rule is complete, it is replaced by the corresponding left side. But matters are more interesting for MERGE rules, which have two constituents on their right sides. Because the first argument s of MERGE1 is lexical, it is always the left corner of that rule. But for MERGE2 and MERGE3, either argument can have moved elements that appear to the right, so which argument is the left corner depends on the particular grammar and even sometimes on the particular derivation.

In the derivation shown in Figure 1, for example, there is one application of MERGE3, to combine *likes* with *what*, and in that case, the selectee lexical item *what* is the left corner because it is the 4th terminal element, while its sister in the derivation tree is terminal element 7. In Figure 2, we can see that $\perp$ occurs first in the input, and is processed in the very first step of the successful left corner parse, even though it is the deepest, rightmost element in the derivation tree.

The MERGE3 rule of MGs raises another tricky issue. After the output of this rule with the predicted right corner is computed, we need to remember it, sometimes for a number of steps, since left and right corners can be arbitrarily far apart. Even with the simple G1, we can get *Aca knows what Bibi knows Aca knows Bibi knows...Aca likes*. We could put the MERGE3 output into a special store, like the HOLD register of ATNs (Wanner and Maratsos, 1978), but here we adopt the equivalent strategy of keeping MERGE3 predictions in the memory that holds our other completed left corners and predicted elements. We call this memory a queue, since it is ordered like a stack, but the parser can access elements that are not on top, as explained below. Queue could be treated as a multiset (since elements can be accessed even if they are not on the top) but treating queue as an ordered structure allows easier definition of oracle and easier definition of which constituent is triggering the next parser's operation.

It will be convenient to number string positions as usual: *0 Aca 1 knows 2 what 3 Bibi 4 likes 5.* Substrings can then be given by their spans, so *Aca* in our example is represented by 0-1, *knows* is 1-2, and an initial empty element would have the span 0-0.

So the parser state is given by

(remaining input, current position, queue),

and we begin with

(input, 0, ϵ).

For any input of length n, we then attempt to apply the LC rules to get

(ϵ, n, 0-n·c),

where · is any type and c is the start category. The LC rules are these:

(0) The SHIFT rule takes an initial (possibly empty) element w with span x-y from the beginning of the remaining input, where the lexicon has $w :: \gamma$, and puts x-y::γ onto the queue.

(1) For an MG rule R of the form $A \leftarrow B\ C$ with left corner B, if an instance of B is on top of the queue, lc1(R) removes B from the top of the queue and replaces it with an element $C \Rightarrow A$. Since any merge rule can have the selector as its left corner, we have the LC rules LC1(MERGE1), LC1(MERGE2), and LC1(MERGE3).

Let's be more precise about being 'an instance'. When R is $A \leftarrow B\ C$, the top element B' of the queue is **an instance of** B iff we can find a (most general) substitution θ such that $B'\theta = B\theta$. In that case, lc(R) replaces B' with $(C \Rightarrow A)\theta$. This computation of substitutions can be done by standard unification (Lloyd, 1987). For example, looking at MERGE1 in Table 1, note that the first constituent on the right specifies the feature f, the sequence γ, and the string s, but not the string t or the 0 or more moving chains $\alpha_1, \ldots, \alpha_k$. So when LC1(MERGE1) applies, the unspecified elements are left as variables, to be instantiated by later steps. So when $s :: =f\gamma$ (for some particular s, f, γ) is on top of the queue, LC1(MERGE1) replaces it by

$$(\underline{t} : f, \alpha_1, \ldots, \alpha_k \Rightarrow s\underline{t} : \gamma, \alpha_1, \ldots, \alpha_k).$$

where underlined elements are variables.

(2) For an MG rule R of the form $A \leftarrow B\ C'$ with completed left corner C and $C\theta = C'\theta$, lc2(R) replaces C on top of the queue by $(B \Rightarrow A)\theta$. For this case, where the second argument on the right side is the left corner, we have the LC rules LC2(MERGE2) and LC2(MERGE3).

(3) Similarly for MG rules $A \leftarrow B$, the only possible leftcorner is a constituent B where $B\theta = B'\theta$, replacing B' by $A\theta$. So we have LC1(MOVE1) and LC1(MOVE2) in this case.

(4) We have introduced 8 LC rules so far. There is SHIFT, and there are 7 LC rules corresponding to the 5 MG rules in Table 1, because of the fact that the left corner of MERGE2 and MERGE3 can be either the first or second element on the right side of the rule. Each LC rule acts to put something new on top of the queue. The 'arc-eager' variant of LC parsing, which we will define here, adds additional variants of those 8 rules: instead of just putting the new element on top of the queue, the element created by a rule can also be used to complete a prediction on the queue, 'connecting' the new element with structure already built.[1] Importantly, the following completion variants of the LC rules can search below the top element to find connecting elements:

c(R) If LC rule R creates a constituent B, and the queue has $B' \Rightarrow A$, where $B\theta = B'\theta$, then c(R) removes $B' \Rightarrow A$ puts $A\theta$ onto the queue.

c1(R) If LC rule R creates $B \Rightarrow A$ and we already have $C \Rightarrow B'$ on the queue, where $B\theta = B'\theta$, then c1(R) removes $C \Rightarrow B'$ and puts $(C \Rightarrow A)\theta$ onto the queue.

c2(R) If LC rule R creates $C \Rightarrow B$ and we already have $B' \Rightarrow A$ on the queue, where $B\theta = B'\theta$, c2(R) removes $B' \Rightarrow A$ and puts $(C \Rightarrow A)\theta$ onto the queue.

c3(R) If LC rule R creates a constituent $C \Rightarrow B$ and we already have $B' \Rightarrow A$ and $D \Rightarrow C'$ on the queue, where $B\theta = B'\theta$ and $C\theta = C'\theta$ c3(R) removes $B' \Rightarrow A$ and $D \Rightarrow C'$ and puts $(D \Rightarrow A)\theta$ onto the queue.

These completion rules are similar to the 'composition' rules of combinatory categorial grammar (Steedman, 2014).

---

[1] Instead of requiring completions to happen when an element is added to the queue, the 'arc-standard' variant of LC parsing uses separate complete rules, which means that a constituent need not (and sometimes cannot) be connected to predicted structure at the time when it is first proposed.

That completes the specification of an arc-eager left corner parser for MGs. The rules are non-deterministic; that is, at many points in a parse, various different LC rules can apply. But for each n-node derivation tree, there is a unique sequence of n LC rule applications that accepts the derived string. This 1-1 correspondence between derivations and parses is unsurprising given the definition of LC. Intuitively, every LC rule _is_ an MG rule, except that it's triggered by its left corner, and it can 'complete' already predicted constituents. This makes it relatively easy to establish the correctness of the parsing method (§5, below).

The 14 node derivation tree in Figure 1 has this 14 step LC parse, indicating the rule used, the remaining input, and queue contents from top to bottom, with variables _M and _N for chain sequences, _Fs for features, _ for span positions, and [] represents the remaining input ϵ in the last 2 steps of the listing:

```
 1. shift [Aca,knows,what,Bibi,likes]
      0-0::=v c
 2. lc1(merge1) [Aca,knows,what,Bibi,likes]
      (0-_.v _M  =>  0-_:c _M)
 3. shift [knows,what,Bibi,likes]
      0-1::d
      (0-_.v _M  =>  0-_:c _M)
 4. c1(lc2(merge2)) [knows,what,Bibi,likes]
      (1-_:=d v _M  =>  0-_:c _M)
 5. shift [what,Bibi,likes]
      1-2::=c =d v
      (1-_:=d v _M  =>  0-_:c _M)
 6. c1(lc1(merge1)) [what,Bibi,likes]
      (2-_.c _M  =>  0-_:c _M)
 7. shift [Bibi,likes]
      2-3::d -wh
      (2-_.c _M  =>  0-_:c _M)
 8. lc2(merge3) [Bibi,likes]
      (_-_.=d _Fs_M  =>  _-_:_Fs,2-3:-wh )
      (2-_.c _M  =>  0-_:c _M)
 9. shift [Bibi,likes]
      3-3::=v +wh c
      (_-_.=d _Fs  =>  _-_:_Fs,2-3:-wh )
      (2-_.c _M  =>  0-_:c _M)
10. lc1(merge1) [Bibi,likes]
      (3-_.v _M  =>  3-_:+wh c _M)
      (_-_.=d _Fs  =>  _-_:_Fs,2-3:-wh )
      (2-_.c _N  =>  0-_:c _N)
11. shift [likes]
      3-4::d
      (3-_.v _M  =>  3-_:+wh c _M)
      (_-_.=d _Fs  =>  _-_:_Fs,2-3:-wh )
      (2-_.c _N  =>  0-_:c _N)
12. c3(lc2(merge2)) [likes]
      (4-_.=d =d v  =>  3-_:+wh c ,2-3:-wh )
      (2-_.c _M  =>  0-_:c _M)
13. c(shift) []
      3-5:+wh c ,2-3:-wh
      (2-_.c _M  =>  0-_:c _M)
14. c(lc1(move1)) []
      0-5:c
```

The derivation tree in Figure 2 has 17 nodes,

and so there is a corresponding 17 step LC parse. For lack of space, we do not present that parse here. It is easy to calculate by hand (especially if you cheat by looking at the tree in Figure 2), but much easier to calculate using an implementation of the parsing method.[2]

4 A left corner oracle

The description of the parsing method above specifies the steps that can be taken, but does not specify which step to take in situations where more than one is possible. As in the case of CFG parsing methods, we could take some sequence of steps arbitrarily and then backtrack, if necessary, to explore other options, but this is not efficient, in general (Aho and Ullman, 1972). A better alternative is to use 'memoization', 'tabling' – that is, keep computed results in an indexed chart or table so that they do not need to be recomputed – compare (Kanazawa, 2008; Swift and Warren, 2012). Another strategy is to compute a beam of most probable alternatives (Manning and Carpenter, 1997). But here, we will show how to define an oracle which can tell us that certain steps cannot possibly lead to completed derivations, following similar work on CFGs (Pereira and Shieber, 1987, §6.3.1). This oracle can be used with memoizing or beam strategies, but as in prior work on CFG parsing, we find that sometimes an easily computed oracle makes even backtracking search efficient. Here we define a simple oracle that suffices for G1 and G2. For each grammar, we can efficiently compute a _link_ relation that we use in this way: A new constituent A' or $B' \Rightarrow A'$ can be put onto the queue only if A' stands in the LINK relation to a _predicted category_, that is, where the start category is predicted when the queue is empty, and a category B is predicted when we have $B \Rightarrow A$ on top of the queue. For many grammars, this use of a LINK oracle eliminates many blind alleys, sometimes infinite ones.

Let LINK(X, Y) hold iff at least one of these conditions holds: (1) X is a left corner of Y, (2) Y contains a initial licensee -f and the first feature of Y is +f, or (3) X and Y are in the transitive closure of the relation defined by (1) and (2). To keep things finite and simple, the elements related by LINK are like queue elements except the mover

---

[2] An implementation of this parser and our example grammars is provided at https://github.com/stanojevic/Left-Corner-MG-parser

lists are always variables, and spans are always un-specified. Clearly, for any grammar, this LINK relation is easy to compute. Possible head feature sequences are non-empty suffixes of lexical features, suffixes that do not begin with -f. The possible left corners of those head sequences are computable from the 7 left corner rules above. This simple LINK relation is our oracle.

5 Correctness, and explicit trees

We sketch the basic ideas needed to demonstrate the soundness of our parsing method (every successful parse is of a grammatical string) and its completeness (every grammatical string has a successful parse). Notice that while the top-down MG parser in Stabler (2013) needed indices to keep track of relative linear positions of predicted constituents, no such thing is needed in the LC parser. This is because in LC parsing, every rule has a bottom-up left corner, and in all cases except for MERGE3, that left corner determines the linear order of any predicted sisters.

For MERGE3, neither element on the right side of the rule, neither the selector nor the selectee, determines the relative position of the other. But the MERGE3 **selectee** has a feature sequence of the form: fγ-g, and this tells us that the linear position of this element will be to the left of the corresponding +g constituent that is the left corner of move1. That is where the string part of the -g constituent 'lands'. The Shortest Move Constraint (SMC) guarantees that this pairing of the +g and -g constituents is unique in any well formed derivation, and the well-formedness of the derivation is guaranteed by requiring that constituents built by the derivation are connected by instances of the 5 MG rules in Table 1.

Locating the relevant +g move1 constituent also sufficiently locates the MERGE3 **selector** with its feature sequence of the form =fγ. It can come from anywhere in the +g move1 constituent's derivation that is compatible with its features. Consequently, when predicting this element, the prediction is put onto the queue when the +g constituent is built, where the compose rules can use it in any feature-compatible position.

With these policies there is a 1-1 correspondence between parses and derivations. In fact, since all variables are instantiated after all substitutions have applied, we can get the LC parser to construct an explicit representation of the corre-sponding derivation tree simply by adding tree arguments to the syntactic features of any grammar, as in (Pereira and Shieber, 1987, §6.1.2). For example, we can augment G1 with derivation tree arguments as follows, writing R/L for trees where R is root and L a list of subtrees, where • is merge and ○ is move, and single capital letters are variables:

```
ε :: =v(V)  c(•/[ε::=v c/[],V])
ε :: =v(V) +wh  c(o/[•/[ε::=v c/[],V]])
knows :: =c(C) =d(D)  v(•/[•/[knows::=c =d v/[],C],D])
likes :: =d(E) =d(D)  v(•/[•/[likes::=d =d v/[],E],D])
Aca :: d(Aca::d/[])
Bibi :: d(Bibi::d/[])
what :: d(what::d -wh/[]) -wh
```

Without any change in the LC method above, with this grammar, the final start category in the last step of the LC parse of *Aca knows what Bibi likes* will have as its argument an explicit representation of the derivation tree of Figure 1, but with binary internal nodes replaced by • and unary ones by ○.

A slightly different version of G1 will build the the derived X-bar tree for the example in Figure 1, or any other string in the infinite language of G1:

```
ε :: =v(V)  c(cP/[c/[ε/[],V]])
ε :: =v(V) +wh(W)  c(cP/[W,c'/[c/[ε/[]],V]])
knows :: =c(C) =d(D)  v(vP/[D,v'/[v/[knows/[]],C]])
likes :: =d(E) =d(D)  v(vP/[D,v'/[v/[likes/[]],E]])
Aca :: d(dP/[Aca/[]])
Bibi :: d(dP/[Bibi/[]])
what :: d(dP(I)/[]) -wh(dP(I)/[what/[]])
```

Notice how this representation of the grammar uses a variable I to coindex the moved element with its original position. In the X-bar tree of Figure 1, that variable is instantiated to 0. Note also how the variable W gets bound to the moved element, so that it appears in under cP, that is, where the moving constituent 'lands'. See e.g. Stabler (2013, Appendix B) for an accessible discussion of how this kind of X-bar structure is related to the derivation, and see Kobele et al. (2007) for technical details. (See footnote 2 for an implementation of the approach presented here.)

6 Conclusions and future work

This paper defines left-corner MG parsing. It is non-deterministic, leaving the question of how to search for a parse. As in context free LC parsing, when there are empty left corners, backtracking search is not guaranteed to terminate. So we could use memoization or a beam or both. All of these search strategies are improved by discarding intermediate results which cannot contribute to a completed parse, and so we define a very simple oracle which does this. That oracle suffices to make backtrack LC parsing of G1 and G2 feasible (see footnote 2). For grammars with empty left corners, stronger oracles can also be formulated, e.g. fully specifying all features and testing spans for emptiness. But for empty left corners, probably the left corner parser is not the best choice. Other ways of mixing top-down and bottom-up can be developed too, for the whole range of generalized left corner methods (Demers, 1977), some of which might be more appropriate for models of human parsing than LC (Johnson and Roark, 2000; Hale, 2014).

As noted earlier, Hunter (2017) aims to define a parser that appropriately models certain aspects of human sentence parsing. In particular, there is some evidence that, in hearing or reading a sentence from beginning to end, humans are inclined to assume that movements are as short as possible – "active gap-filling". It looks like the present model has a structure which would allow for modeling this preference in something like the way Hunter proposes, but we have not tried to capture that or any other human preferences here. Our goal here has been just to design a simple left-corner mechanism that does exactly what an arbitrary MG requires. Returning to Hunter's project with this simpler model will hopefully contribute to the project of moving toward more reasonable models of human linguistics performance.

There are many other natural extensions of these ideas:

- The proposed definition of LC parsing is designed to make correctness transparent, but now that the idea is clear, some simplifications will be possible. In particular, it should be possible to eliminate explicit unification, and to eliminate spans in stack elements.

- The LC parser could also be extended to other types of MG rules proposed for head-movement, adjunction, coordination, copying, etc. (Torr and Stabler, 2016; Fowlie, 2014; Gärtner and Michaelis, 2010; Kobele, 2006).

- Our LC method could also be adapted to multiple context free grammars (MCFGs) which are expressively equivalent, and to other closely related systems (Seki et al., 1991; Kallmeyer, 2010).

- Stanojević (2017) shows how bottom-up transition-based parsers can be provided for MGs, and those allow LSTMs and other neural systems to be trained as oracles (Lewis et al., 2016). It would be interesting to explore similar oracles for slightly more predictive methods like LC, and trained on recently built MGbank (Torr, 2018).

- For her 'geometric' neural realizations of MG derivations (Gerth and beim Graben, 2012), Gerth (2015, p.78) says she would have used an LC MG parser in her neural modeling if one had been available, so that kind of project could be revisited.

We leave these to future work.

Acknowledgments

The first author is supported by ERC H2020 Advanced Fellowship GA 742137 SEMANTAX grant. The authors are grateful to Tim Hunter for sharing the early version of his LC paper and to Mark Steedman for support in developing and presenting this work.

References

Steven P. Abney and Mark Johnson. 1991. Memory requirements and local ambiguities of parsing strategies. *Journal of Psycholinguistic Research* 20:233–249.

Alfred V. Aho and Jeffrey D. Ullman. 1972. *The Theory of Parsing, Translation, and Compiling. Volume 1: Parsing*. Prentice-Hall, Englewood Cliffs, New Jersey.

Joan Bresnan, Ronald M. Kaplan, Stanley Peters, and Annie Zaenen. 1982. Cross-serial dependencies in Dutch. *Linguistic Inquiry* 13(4):613–635.

Noam Chomsky. 1995. *The Minimalist Program*. MIT Press, Cambridge, Massachusetts.

Alan J. Demers. 1977. Generalized left corner parsing. In *4th Annual ACM Symposium on Principles of Programming Languages*. pages 170–181.

Hans den Besten and Gert Webelhuth. 1990. Stranding. In G. Grewendorf and W. Sternefeld, editors, *Scrambling and Barriers*, Academic Press, NY.

Victor J. Díaz, Vicente Carillo, and Miguel A. Alonso. 2002. A left corner parser for tree adjoining grammars. In *Proceedings of the Sixth International Workshop on Tree Adjoining Grammar and Related Frameworks (TAG+6)*. Association for Computational Linguistics, pages 90–95. http://www.aclweb.org/anthology/W02-2213.

Meaghan Fowlie. 2014. Adjunction and minimalist grammars. In G. Morrill, R. Muskens, R. Osswald, and F. Richter, editors, *Formal Grammar: 19th International Conference*. Springer, NY, pages 34–51.

Hans-Martin Gärtner and Jens Michaelis. 2010. On the treatment of multiple wh-interrogatives in minimalist grammars. In Thomas Hanneforth and Gisbert Fanselow, editors, *Language and Logos: Studies in Theoretical and Computational Linguistics*, Academie Verlag, Berlin, pages 339–366.

Sabrina Gerth. 2015. *Memory limitations in sentence comprehension*. Universitätsverlag, Potsdam.

Sabrina Gerth and Peter beim Graben. 2012. Geometric representations for minimalist grammars. *Journal of Logic, Language and Information* 21(4):393–432.

Thomas Graf, Alëna Aksënova, and Aniello De Santo. 2016. A single movement normal form for minimalist grammars. In A. Foret, G. Morrill, R. Muskens, R. Osswald, and S. Pogodalla, editors, *Formal Grammar: 20th and 21st International Conferences, Revised Selected Papers*. Springer, Berlin, LNCS 9804, pages 200–215.

Günther Grewendorf, editor. 2015. *Remnant Movement*. Mouton de Gruyter, NY.

John T. Hale. 2014. *Automaton Theories of Human Sentence Comprehension*. CSLI, Stanford.

Henk Harkema. 2001a. A characterization of minimalist languages. In P. de Groote, G. Morrill, and C. Retoré, editors, *Logical Aspects of Computational Linguistics*. Springer, NY, LNCS 2099, pages 193–211.

Henk Harkema. 2001b. *Parsing Minimalist Languages*. Ph.D. thesis, University of California, Los Angeles.

Roland Hinterhölzl. 2006. *Scrambling, Remnant Movement, and Restructuring in West Germanic*. Oxford University Press, NY.

Tim Hunter. 2017. Left-corner parsing of minimalist grammars. Technical report, UCLA. Forthcoming.

Mark Johnson and Brian Roark. 2000. Compact non-left-recursive grammars using the selective left-corner transform and factoring. In *Proceedings of the 18th International Conference on Computational Linguistics, COLING*. pages 355–361.

Laura Kallmeyer. 2010. *Parsing Beyond Context-Free Grammars*. Springer, NY.

Makoto Kanazawa. 2008. A prefix correct Earley recognizer for multiple context free grammars. In *Proceedings of the 9th International Workshop on Tree Adjoining Grammars and Related Formalisms*. pages 49–56.

Richard S. Kayne. 1994. *The Antisymmetry of Syntax*. MIT Press, Cambridge, Massachusetts.

Gregory M. Kobele. 2006. *Generating Copies: An Investigation into Structural Identity in Language and Grammar*. Ph.D. thesis, UCLA.

Gregory M. Kobele. 2010. Without remnant movement, MGs are context-free. In C. Ebert, G. Jäger, and J. Michaelis, editors, *Mathematics of Language 10/11*. Springer, NY, LNCS 6149, pages 160–173.

Gregory M. Kobele, Christian Retoré, and Sylvain Salvati. 2007. An automata-theoretic approach to minimalism. In James Rogers and Stephan Kepser, editors, *Model Theoretic Syntax at 10. ESSLLI'07 Workshop Proceedings*.

Hilda Koopman and Anna Szabolcsi. 2000. *Verbal Complexes*. MIT Press, Cambridge, Massachusetts.

Mike Lewis, Kenton Lee, and Luke Zettlemoyer. 2016. LSTM CCG parsing. In *Proceedings of the 15th Annual Conference of the North American Chapter of the Association for Computational Linguistics*.

John W. Lloyd. 1987. *Foundations of Logic Programming*. Springer, Berlin.

Christopher D. Manning and Bob Carpenter. 1997. Probabilistic parsing using left corner language models. In *Proceedings of the 1997 International Workshop on Parsing Technologies*. Reprinted in H. Bunt and A. Nijholt (eds.) *Advances in Probabilistic and Other Parsing Technologies*, Boston, Kluwer: pp. 105-124. Also available as arXiv:cmp-lg/9711003.

Jens Michaelis. 2001. Transforming linear context free rewriting systems into minimalist grammars. In P. de Groote, G. Morrill, and C. Retoré, editors, *Logical Aspects of Computational Linguistics*. Springer, NY, LNCS 2099, pages 228–244.

Fernando C. N. Pereira and Stuart M. Shieber. 1987. *Prolog and Natural Language Analysis*. CSLI, Stanford.

Philip Resnik. 1992. Left-corner parsing and psychological plausibility. In *Proceedings of the 14th International Conference on Computational Linguistics, COLING 92*. pages 191–197.

D. J. Rosenkrantz and P. M. Lewis. 1970. Deterministic left corner parsing. In *IEEE Conference Record of the 11th Annual Symposium on Switching and Automata Theory*. pages 139–152.

Hiroyuki Seki, Takashi Matsumura, Mamoru Fujii, and Tadao Kasami. 1991. On multiple context-free grammars. *Theoretical Computer Science* 88:191–229.

Stuart M. Shieber. 1985. Evidence against the context-freeness of natural language. *Linguistics and Philosophy* 8(3):333–344.

Edward P. Stabler. 1997. Derivational minimalism. In C. Retoré, editor, *Logical Aspects of Computational Linguistics*, Springer-Verlag, NY, LNCS 1328, pages 68–95.

Edward P. Stabler. 2011. Computational perspectives on minimalism. In Cedric Boeckx, editor, *Oxford Handbook of Linguistic Minimalism*, Oxford University Press, Oxford, pages 617–641.

Edward P. Stabler. 2013. Two models of minimalist, incremental syntactic analysis. *Topics in Cognitive Science* 5(3):611–633.

Miloš Stanojević. 2017. Minimalist grammar transition-based parsing. In *International Conference on Logical Aspects of Computational Linguistics, LACL*. Springer, LNCS 10054, pages 273–290.

Mark J. Steedman. 2014. Categorial grammar. In A. Carnie, Y. Sato, and D. Siddiqi, editors, *Routledge Handbook of Syntax*, Routledge, NY, pages 670–701.

Terrance Swift and David S. Warren. 2012. XSB: Extending prolog with tabled logic programming. *Theory and Practice of Logic Programming* 12(1-2):157–187. ArXiv:1012.5123.

Gary Thoms and George Walkden. 2018. vP-fronting with and without remnant movement. *Journal of Linguistics* pages 1–54.

John Torr. 2018. Constraining mgbank: Agreement, l-selection and supertagging in minimalist grammars. In *Proceedings of the 56th Annual Meeting on Association for Computational Linguistics*. Association for Computational Linguistics, Melbourne, Australia.

John Torr and Edward Stabler. 2016. Coordination in minimalist grammars. In *Proceedings of the 12th Annual Workshop on Tree-Adjoining Grammars and Related Formalisms, TAG+*.

Gertjan van Noord. 1991. Head corner parsing for discontinuous constituency. In *Proceedings of the 29th Annual Meeting on Association for Computational Linguistics*. Association for Computational Linguistics, Stroudsburg, PA, USA, ACL 1991, pages 114–121.

Eric Wanner and Michael P. Maratsos. 1978. An ATN approach to comprehension. In M. Halle, J. Bresnan, and G. A. Miller, editors, *Linguistic Theory and Psychological Reality*, MIT Press, Cambridge, Massachusetts.

Author Index

Association for Computational Linguistics
209 N. Eighth Street
Stroudsburg, Pennsylvania 18360

ISBN 978-1-5108-6715-4